Making Wall Street Irrelevant
Successful Investing Made Simple

By
Mark Bern, CFA

Table of Contents

Introduction

A favorite quote from Warren Buffett is from his Letter to Shareholders in the 2016 Berkshire Hathaway annual report.

"Charlie and I have no magic plan to add earnings except to dream big and to be prepared mentally and financially to act fast when opportunities present themselves. Every decade or so, dark clouds will fill the economic skies, and they will briefly rain gold. When downpours of that sort occur, it's imperative that we rush outdoors carrying washtubs, not teaspoons."

Feb. 25, 2017

What he is talking about is when the markets crash, it is important to have enough cash on hand to take advantage of all the great opportunities that become available. Timing your entry point is a key to successful long-term investing. It may not be a market crash, but maybe a great company has a bad quarter or year that drags its value down into bargain territory. Having money available to invest when that happens is just as important. In other words, cash is not trash in Mr. Warren's view, nor mine.

A few years ago, I wrote an immensely popular series of articles on the investor site Seeking Alpha about how I created my own portfolio over a lifetime. As time passed, I continually refined my approach, and since so much has changed due to the pandemic, I thought a refresher was in order. And what better way to do that than by authoring a book, as many of my readers suggested.

How did people with take-home pay (after taxes) of less than $50,000 per year (in today's dollars after adjusting for inflation) pay their bills AND end up with $5 million or more in savings? They did it over a lifetime. This book provides answers to this mystery and explains how most people can do the same.

As the old cliché goes, time in the market is more important than timing the market. Time and patience are key elements to successful investing. Other key ingredients are selectivity and consistency. How to apply each will be discussed in detail.

This book is meant to provide a guide for investors of all ages, to help each of them determine reasonable goals and develop a plan to attain those goals over their respective remaining investing lifetimes. I spend much of my time during retirement now authoring articles to explain complex concepts in simple, easy-to-understand language that anyone can understand. That is my primary goal: taking the fear out of investing by explaining a step-by-step approach that anyone can follow and use to achieve success.

Obviously, there are many ways to build an investment portfolio and allocate funds across different classes of assets. The method described here is how I have learned over a lifetime what works best for me, and I believe it can work for anyone. Having a set of simple, straightforward principles and specific goals can help one stay on the right path, and my hope is that my explanations will help readers formulate a similar system of investing that works for them.

The approach I explain in this book is intended to provide a flexible set of guidelines that can be modified to fit any investor's needs. Three systematic methods of adding investments will be included.

They are proven to work over the long term. Most folks think that these strategies only apply to stocks, but, as you will see, they are useful tools for investing in almost any type of asset.

What are the distinct types of assets used for investment? The list can get long if we break down each class of asset into its subgroups, like stocks into mutual funds, ETFs (exchange-traded funds), MLPs (master limited partnerships), CEFs (closed-end funds), etc. I will describe the subgroup(s) that I prefer in each asset class and explain why I like it. But for now, I will list only the major asset classes that I consider to be easily investable for the average person: stocks, bonds, real estate, and precious metals. I do not cover things like collectibles, art, or digital coins (like Bitcoin or Ethereum) because I have found that those items tend to be too speculative for the average investor. Mine is a very conservative approach to building a retirement nest egg. Commodities are very cyclical, and investors can use mining or exploration companies' stocks to invest indirectly when values become enticing.

I will go into detail about how to understand your investment horizon(s) and why it is important, how to value assets of different classes in order to find bargains, using the concept of compound interest to make your money work for you, how I allocate funds between asset classes, why I find it important to invest for a rising income and total return rather than just appreciation, why it is imperative to always have some cash available for emergencies, where I invest my "cash" while I wait for bargains and much more to help develop a lifelong plan to meet your financial needs.

What is Financial Security?

Financial security can mean different things to different people. For most folks, it means not needing to worry about how to make ends meet. To others, it means that they do not need to remain in a job that they hate; rather, they can afford to follow their passion to work in a field that they enjoy without the worry of how to pay the bills. For me, it has always meant that I could work if I wanted but didn't have to for the money. I may not be rich, but the income my wife and I have coming in automatically pays the bills and allows us to save a little more each month. Or we can splurge on something every now and then without worrying about a budget. It is a nice feeling.

Most financial gurus and advisors will tell you that you need a certain amount of savings to be financially secure. Today, I believe the number going around is $2.6 million. The problem is that financial security is not guaranteed based on how much money you have. It is based on how much income you have before you get out of bed each day. Savings can provide a good income if invested properly over the long term but can also drop precipitously during market crashes. How secure would you feel if your $2.6 million suddenly turned into $1.3 million? It happens. It happened in 2007-2009. The market fell about 57%, from top to bottom, during that period. The S&P 500 Index fell by over 37% in a few weeks during 2020. It dropped 48% in 1974-75. It fell 47% in 2000-2002. It fell 33% in 1987.

Of course, the market always rebounds and eventually makes new highs, but if you depend on growth stocks to fund your retirement, it gets scary every time the market drops. If you do not pull too much out to live on during the down periods, you could be fine. However, if you are withdrawing 4% each year from a depleted balance, suddenly, you will need to achieve over 100% gains just to get back to where you once were.

My belief (based on my experience) is that there is a better way. By building up layers of dependable income, growing consistently over a lifetime, you will never need to worry about what the market is doing. It will not matter. By selecting quality stocks that pay dividends that rise every year, all you need to do is watch your income grow until it hits your goal. It sounds simple, but the process is a little more complicated. This book is designed to simplify the process and keep readers from straying off the proven path to financial security.

Setting Reasonable Goals and Milestones

If you are just starting out on your investment adventures, it is important to establish a plan with reasonable, achievable goals and intermediate milestones. Even if you are well into the adventure, it is never too late to start using milestones and setting a long-term goal (explained in detail in Chapter 3). I suggest only focusing on the next milestone to alleviate the inevitable frustration that creeps in upon setbacks (which are a natural part of investing).

Each milestone is within reach in a few years, so it is always achievable if you stick to the plan. Once one milestone is achieved, just plod on toward the next one. Success breeds more success. Never get too aggressive with your goals or milestones. Keeping milestones achievable within a reasonable time is important. It allows one to enjoy the sweet taste of success repeatedly at regular intervals. That, in turn, helps you to stay on the course, knowing that the next milestone (and time for celebration) is coming and that you CAN make it happen again and again just like you did the last time. The more success you enjoy, the more motivated you will be to keep doing what works without deviating from the plan. The most important milestone is always the next one. It is remarkably similar to team sports. Concentrate on the present and proceed toward the future one step at a time. You cannot win the championship (your ultimate goal) unless you win the game you are in right now (your next milestone).

One of my guiding principles for investing (which you can find in Appendix A) is to invest like a millionaire (maybe I should have used billionaire since a million dollars does not buy as much today as it did in the past). I will continually emphasize this concept because it really is that important and because this approach is rarely understood by most investors. It leads to lower risk and overall higher long-term returns. Of course, there are specific investing vehicles available to the extremely wealthy of which we mortals cannot take advantage. But, just the same, the underlying concept still applies, and I believe you will find it useful.

Every investor (whether great or average) had to start somewhere, even Warren Buffett (whose foundational principles will be emphasized). As many great investors will remind us, "It only takes a few excellent investments to keep a portfolio growing." In other words, you do not need to hit home runs with every swing. Lots of singles coupled with an occasional homer will do just fine.

When to Start Preparing for Retirement

Many people do not give retirement any thought until they reach their forties or fifties. That makes the preparation much more difficult. Something to keep in mind is the fact that the greatest amount of accumulation occurs during the last ten years of your working life. But that only applies because of the impact of compounding. If you wait ten years from now to start, your best ten years of accumulation will pale in comparison to what could have been. It could mean hundreds of thousands of dollars less (or even a million dollars or more for some). Is it worth it to have things today that you could have lived happily without for a few years until they fit into your budget more affordably? Living within your budget today can make a dramatic difference when the time comes to retire later. It may mean the difference between retiring on your own terms or having to work several years longer than you would like. When should you start preparing for retirement? No matter what age you are, the answer is always now. The sooner you start, the less painful it will be over your lifetime, especially the nearer you get to retirement age. You do not need to start saving large amounts to begin with; just start with something on a regular basis and watch it grow slowly at first and then at an ever-increasing rate.

It is amazing just how much accumulation goes on after the first 20 years of investing and even more so after 30 years. That is when it gets really interesting!

Time Horizon, Strategy, and Diversification of Risk

What is your time horizon? That is something most people do not give enough thought to when planning for retirement. You will need your nest egg to last another 20-30 years (and perhaps longer) after you retire. You need to consider what inflation could do to the purchasing power of your retirement income and how to stay ahead of it. Make sure your goals align with your needs. This book will address these issues and many others.

In the following chapters, I will lay out my strategy for investing, primarily in equities but including real estate, fixed income (bonds, CDs, etc.), and commodities (including precious metals) that I have developed over a lifetime. For me, investing is more of a process of elimination using a rules-based selection process that guides me to the best investment for long-term appreciation and income. There will also be short interludes throughout the book referring to real-life examples of ordinary people who amassed millions of dollars in wealth without anyone noticing. When they died, each one left behind a fortune for the benefit of heirs and/or favorite charities. These were people with a plan who stuck to it year after year. They were also people in average jobs with no special advantages; they were the sort of people to which I can relate, and you should too. My investment philosophy has been inspired over the years by comparable stories. I trust that my words may become your inspiration.

Part I:
A Unique Approach to Investing
in a Complicated World

Chapter 1:
A Little Personal Background
for Perspective

When I was in my 20s and just out of college, I set a goal to save $25,000. Back then (in the 1970s), that was a lot of money for someone that age (about $141,000 today)[1]. I attained that goal within four years. My next goal was to double it to $50,000, then $100,000, and each milestone thereafter was to add another $100,000. In looking back, those goals were just milestones leading to the ultimate goal of financial security and independence. I did not know how much I would need for retirement at the time, so I simply set a new milestone each time one was achieved. One of the best things about having a plan and sticking to it is that it gets easier to achieve with each new milestone, especially after hitting $300,000 because from that point forward, your contributions will become a smaller factor in your quest for financial freedom. Your money is working with you and for you to achieve each new milestone, and once you hit that milestone, it becomes much easier to attain all future milestones. Or, at least, it should be if you are investing correctly. I must admit here that I strayed from the path a few times and got behind as I still had a lot to learn. My sincere aim in writing this book is to help others avoid many of the pitfalls that I encountered along the way.

My biggest hindrances were my lack of knowledge and the naïve expectation that I could beat the average investor while accepting too much risk. Believe me, experience and knowledge have helped me to reduce my short-term goals and remain more focused on the path toward longer-term goals.

As stated in another way, successful investing is not winning the lottery; it is finding a proven strategy that has worked for millions of other individuals throughout history and sticking with it through good times and bad. The good news is that there is more than one strategy that will work; you just need to find the one that you can stick with over a lifetime and make it work for you.

In my twenties, I was good at saving, but the investing part was not my forte. That came with experience and a lot of study and training, not necessarily in that order. Initially, I accepted more risk than I needed to in the hope that I could achieve those milestones faster. In contrast to the now-famous quote of Mr. Gecko from the movie, "Wall Street," greed is not good for most investors. It generally leads to greater inconsistency and too many unnecessary setbacks. If you win, you win big, but when you lose, you lose big! When an investor loses 50 percent of his or her portfolio s/he will need a gain of 100 percent just to get back to even. Never forget that! My number one rule is to limit losses. I believe someone else of greater fame with the initials W.B. (Warren Buffett, also known as the Oracle of Omaha) has been quoted in a similar fashion.[2]

---

[1] Determined by using an online calculator available at usinflationcalculator.com

[2] https://www.investopedia.com/financial-edge/0210/rules-that-warren-buffett-lives-by.aspx. "Rule No. 1: Never lose money. Rule No. 2: Never forget Rule No. 1."

Learning how to limit or avoid major setbacks is one of the most important keys to successful investing. I will explain how to implement rule number one later in the book.

The point I want to stress here is that it took me more than a decade to realize what I was doing wrong. Then, I read an excerpt from a study that illustrated how more than 40 percent of the total return of the S&P 500 had come from dividends when measured over the exceptionally long term (such as in a typical lifetime of 30 to 50 years of saving and investing). Suddenly, it dawned on me that by looking solely for growth (rather than total return), I could be missing out on as much as 40 percent of the potential return that a stock portfolio could offer. That was revolutionary, and so began the evolution of my investment approach.

Helping friends save for college

One other event happened that helped to shape my investing philosophy. A young married couple expecting a baby (close personal friends) came to me and asked what I would invest in at the time to ensure having enough for the baby's college education when the time came. They had $25,000 they could live without that they wanted to invest for that purpose, and they did not want to invest in stocks. The time was the 1980s when interest rates were sky-high (30-year Treasury bonds hit yields above 14 percent back then)[3]. That was before 529 college funds were established, so they did not have such alternatives to consider. So, I suggested that they consider zero-coupon Treasury bonds or CATS[4] (Certificates of Accrual on Treasury Securities), and they did. I did not. They were happy. I was sad. I was still learning.

Today's equivalent of a CATS bond is a zero-coupon Treasury STRIPS[5] (Separate Trading of Registered Interest and Principal Securities).

The couple was able to lock in a 12.5 percent yield. I also explained to them that they would need to pay taxes on the accrued interest each year, which they agreed would be workable. It was like making an initial investment of $25,000 and adding a bit more each year, but with the assurance that there would be enough to meet the needs of college expenses when needed with truly little downside risk.

The total of those taxes amounted to about another $36,000 spread over the 18-year holding period.

---

[3] https://www.macrotrends.net/2521/30-year-treasury-bond-rate-yield-chart. - Macrotrend.com

[4] https://www.investopedia.com/terms/c/cats.asp Certificate of Accrual on Treasury Securities Overview. - Investopedia.com.

[5] https://www.investopedia.com/terms/t/treasurystrips.asp. Treasury STRIPS (T-Strips) definition and how to invest – Investopedia.com.

By paying the taxes annually on the accrued interest earned (but not received until either maturity or sale), the couple also benefited from paying a lower tax rate than would otherwise have been the case had they had to pay taxes on the full amount of capital gain and accrued interest all at once when they sold the bonds. They would have been in a much higher tax bracket with an extra $180,000 in earnings all in one year. The capital gains tax rate would not have changed either way.

By the time the baby had grown up and was ready for college, those bonds had accumulated over $180,000 in interest. Yields had dropped to more "normal" levels of eight percent, so the price available for the bonds had also increased above face value. Think about this scenario for a moment: $25,000 (plus the $36,000 added over time) turned into more than $250,000 in eighteen years. If they could hold onto those bonds for the full 30-year term, the total value of the bonds, when cashed in, would have been about $856,000. The total taxes paid over the full 30 years would amount to approximately $196,000, so the total investment would have been about $221,000. Upon cashing in the bonds, they would only owe taxes on the final year of interest since the taxes on the accrued interest had been paid as it accrued each year. They would get to keep the entire amount after the final year of taxes to be reinvested toward retirement.

Again, I want you to think about these results. $221,000 invested periodically over a 30-year period turns into $856,000, and the taxes are already paid. You get to keep the full amount, less the taxes due in the final year, on one year of interest. That is the power of compound interest, interest accruing on an investment over time plus interest on the interest. This concept will keep coming up throughout the book because it is another of the keys to successful investing.

The purpose of all this experience chatter is to frame the answer to why I invest the way I do. I invest with a long-term investment horizon, even now at the ripe old age of 75. I need my money to last at least 20 years to provide for my wife and myself. We would also like to leave a nice inheritance for each of our two children to help them in life and to give them a good start on their respective retirement plans. Therefore, my horizon extends beyond my own lifetime and that of my spouse, which is, by definition, long-term. That is how I invest: for the long term and with a rising stream of income for me, my wife, and our children long after we are gone.

The next chapter," Investing Like a Millionaire," gets to the root of my investing philosophy. Once you understand this concept, we can move on to developing a personal plan.

Chapter 2:
Investing Like a Millionaire

Patience is Key

If you want to be a millionaire, you need to invest like one. The ultra-wealthy individuals do not need all the income from their investments. And they certainly are not desperate to increase their income from investments every year. But it just happens anyway without their trying. How? I am glad you asked.

You see, wealthy people can afford to wait for bargains. That is how most of them got wealthy anyway, by buying things cheaply and reselling them for a profit, whether it is through building a company that offers products or services or by identifying distress situations that allow them to buy something that is temporarily out of favor and then reselling it later for much more (such as real estate). Stepping back for a moment, we need to accept one other concept about becoming wealthy: they started saving early so they would have the capacity to buy when bargains arose. The initial capital (money) must come from somewhere. Many wealthy people started small businesses, worked hard, and grew their businesses, creating their wealth. But many others just worked at a job, saved, and invested. Either way, the outcome is the same, but the process is different.

For example, when you start a service business, you begin by offering your own services at a price that includes your wages and overhead expenses. Then, if you are good at what you do, your customers increase in number, and you need to hire employees. The owners are investing some of their profits back into the business in order to expand. You charge the customer one price that includes the employee wages, benefits, and overhead plus a profit for yourself, and you pay the employee a small portion of the billed amount. You paid your employee one amount for his/her services and then charged the customer a larger amount. That, of course, is a simplified version of how real life works, but hopefully, you get the idea. Business owners, large and small, are always looking for ways to reduce costs and increase profits: buy low and sell higher or increase the volume of sales while holding some overhead expenses steady. I could get into a discussion about fixed costs and incremental expenses, but this is not a book about building a business. It is about investing.

The same principles apply to investing, especially for those who are not immediately dependent upon income. This is where my investing philosophy butts heads with the accepted norm espoused by Wall Street. According to the pundits, we must all be fully invested all the time, or we might miss some great rally (especially in the stock market). It is also widely accepted that even if one invests at the top of the market, it will not really matter in the long run. That is ridiculous! It does matter. They would be ahead in the end, but not by as much as if they invested like the rich do.

Wall Street needs us (individual investors) to keep investing all we have because if we do not, they cannot make as much money. Remember that much of the profits flowing into Wall Street come from either fees on assets under management (the more assets you give them to manage, the more Wall Street gets to keep, no matter what happens to your money), margin interest on loans to clients to buy more stocks, interest fees for temporarily loaning out your shares to investors who want to short a stock, and loads (another form of commissions on managed mutual funds paid to salespeople). Of course, they want us all fully invested. That is how they make more money. And you thought Wall Street was run by a group of benevolent people who spend all their time devising ways to "help" the little guy become rich? Right.

So, when does Mr. Rich Guy buy stock in a company he really likes for the long term? After the price has gone through the roof? No. He buys the stock when the company or the overall market hits a speed bump and falls to a level that represents excellent value. After the Financial Crisis of 2008, the market bottomed out at levels not seen since 1996, twelve years earlier. From the 2007 high, it took the broadly based S&P 500 Index until 2013 (six years) to completely recover the former record levels of valuation. Wall Street will point to that recovery and say, "See, it recovered just like we said it would, and you haven't lost a dime." True, but... All you had to do was wait for six years to get back to even. Then Wall Street would say, "If you are a young investor, you are able to take on more risk because you have plenty of time to recover from any setbacks." True again, but do we really want to keep taking these setbacks? Do the wealthy invest at the top? Or do they wait for bargains? If you want to become wealthy, you need to invest the way the wealthy invest.

Another way to look at this: Do you always buy large ticket items (like cars, furniture, appliances, etc.) when there are no incentives, or do you often make such purchases when there is a sale going on? Do you replace your linens and bedding at full price or when those items are on sale for 50% off? It's the same principle. Invest like you are buying a big-ticket item that you need to last for a long time. Investing should be long-term. Anything else is speculating (otherwise known as gambling). And, by the way, if you aren't buying expensive, durable goods when they go on sale, you are probably paying too much.

That extra savings could have gone toward your retirement savings.

How does Warren Buffett Invest?

One obvious way to answer that question is to look at what Warren Buffett (considered one of the greatest investors of all time) does. Is he always fully invested? Rarely, if ever. His Berkshire Hathaway (BRK.A) company accumulates cash year after year, making small investments here and there (huge to us), sitting on a pile of cash in the billions of dollars until he finds a bargain. Currently, Berkshire has more than $330 billion sitting in cash. The bargain does not necessarily have to be after the stock has crashed. It is often a business that is experiencing (or is about to experience) a strong positive trend, often with a little help from Uncle Warren's guidance. The point is that he waits patiently until he finds something that presents a great long-term value.

We all do not have the resources or analytical skills of Warren Buffett, nor do many of us have the time it takes to identify major trends. However, one thing we do have is the ability to recognize a bargain when it is obvious. In 2009 and 2010, after stocks had lost most of the accumulated value gained in the previous decade, it should have been obvious to anyone with some cash sitting on the sideline that bargains were available. But instead, what most small investors were doing was selling because the fear of additional losses was unbearable. Most investors had been following the advice of Wall Street and kept on buying right on up to the top, even after assuming it was not a crash but was "just another dip." The one thing you need to understand is that Wall Street does not care whether you win or lose; it just wants your money to manage so it can keep siphoning off more for its executive bonuses. They are only interested in their own profits, period. Of course, they would like you to make a little more money, but that is not their primary focus.

Who has your best interests at heart?

We need to look out for ourselves. We need to have a plan. We do not need to blindly follow Wall Street's advice. The only one you can trust to do what is best for you is yourself. Okay, that was a little harsh.

There are advisors who truly do want you to do well. But ask this question of yourself. Do advisors only call when an investment represents a great long-term value? Did they call you in 2007? You should understand that if you answered yes to both questions, you got one of them wrong. If your advisor called you and recommended a stock in 2007, s/he was just trying to do their respective jobs and create some commissions, oblivious to the reality of what was about to happen.

The point is this: you can do better without listening to Wall Street. Have you ever noticed that Wall Street Analysts rarely change a rating on a stock from buy to sell until after the price has fallen? Is that the best advice? Is it beneficial? Do not kid yourself into believing that Wall Street is always right. The stock market does go up more often than it goes down. That is a simple truth. Over the long run, Wall Street will eventually be right. They are just playing the odds by always predicting that stocks, bonds, or whatever they are shilling are going to go higher. Most of the time, they will be right simply because of the percentages. That does not require a lot of skill. In fact, it requires no skill at all. A broken watch will be right twice a day. Wall Street will be right often because asset values tend to go up over time. Do not forget that a portion of that rising asset value is just inflation.

Again, Wall Street is merely playing the odds like a casino. A casino skims a small percentage out of the aggregate amount wagered over time. It always wins if it can keep people gambling long enough. Wall Street just wants us all to stay at the gaming tables long enough, too, so it can "earn" a small percentage of what we wager. One of the greatest investing minds of all time, Benjamin Graham, tells us, "In the short term, the market is a voting machine, but in the long run, it is a weighing machine." He was a value investor and Warren Buffett's mentor. The point he was trying to make is that the market can be irrational in the short term but is always rational over the long term. In other words, asset prices can go up to prices far above their true value and far lower, as well, in the short term, but over the long term, prices will always revert to the mean or the real value of future expected cash flows. Maybe not all assets are at the same time, but eventually, each investment will find its true value. It is our job to buy assets when they fall below true value or, as stated another way, when they become bargains.

So, when the price of an asset, be it stocks, bonds, real estate, or commodities, rises to irrational levels, it is better to look elsewhere or patiently wait for a better price.

There may be more skill, in terms of knowledge and experience, on Wall Street than most of us have. But we do not really need that much skill. The thing we need the most is patience. Add a little skill, a solid plan, and a lot of patience, and you will do much better than relying on Wall Street.

Chapter 3:
The Concept of Compounding

Setting Milestones

"Compound interest is the eighth wonder of the world! He who understands it earns it…he who does not…pays it." – Albert Einstein.

I want to begin with a few hypothetical examples to illustrate this concept, and then I will include a real-life example to solidify the importance of this concept in your mind. Most people who have saved over the course of their lives will tell you that the first $100,000 is the hardest. It is the first of any amount that is difficult, no matter what it is, because the hard part is getting started, and the second hardest part is remaining consistent. So, I will start out with a simple example of how you can get to $25,000 in a reasonable time with a household income starting at $31,200. That is where a young man close to me started after his first promotion out of college, so it offers a close resemblance to reality. This example happened a few decades ago, so the numbers should be higher today.

Here are the assumptions. Starting out on the bottom rung in a supervisory position at $31,200 per year (about $15 per hour) with expectations of five percent annual increases in earnings per year throughout a career. Many people do much better than this (I did), and others do not do as well. I just wanted to begin with something that represents an average (or maybe below) income and career. The company offers a 401K plan but does not match employee contributions.

Assumptions about savings by the employee: Contributes 5 percent to 401K in the first year, 7.5 percent in the second year, and 10 percent of wages earned in each year thereafter; opens a Roth IRA and contributes $3,500 in the first two years, then the maximum allowed by law of $5,500 per year (it has now been raised to $7,000) thereafter.

I realize that it may take a lot of people longer to reach those maximums, but that is what I did when my salary was similar, and we lived in Arlington, Virginia, with a newborn baby. I was earning about $35,000, and my wife was working part-time while caring for our baby and earning about $8,000. We had just bought a house for $220,000, and the budget was very tight, but we somehow always found a way to save about 25 percent of our gross income every year. Realistic for some or not, I know it can be done because we did it. Needless to say, we didn't eat out a lot, drink, go to the movies much, or buy expensive clothes, cars, or furniture.

Assumptions about total return: average of 7 percent per year compounded tax deferred. This will vary from year to year, and while the long-term average is somewhat higher, I believe this level is attainable over the next decade if you follow the rules I will outline later in the book.

If it takes you five (or even six) years to achieve your first milestone, it does not matter in the long run. What matters is that you took the first step. It is also important to keep in mind that it gets easier as you hit additional milestones.

Hypothetical Milestone Example

Here is a table that shows the progress toward the first goal of $25,000.

Year	Added/Yr. to IRA	Average Gain	IRA Yr.-end Balance	Added/Yr. to 401K	Average Gain	401K Yr.-end Balance	Total Balance
1	$3,500	$245	$3,745	$1,560	$109	$1,669	$5,414
2	$3,500	$262	$7,507	$2,457	$117	$4,243	$11,750
3	$5,500	$526	$13,533	$3,440	$297	$7,980	$21,513
4	$5,500	$947	$19,980	$3,612	$559	$12,150	$32,130

So, you see how slowly it accumulates in the beginning and how the balance starts to get a little more interesting each year? If everything goes smoothly (which it will not), you will accumulate $25,000 in about 3.3 years. Depending upon how your investments perform and how much you can commit to saving each year, it may take a year or two longer, or it may take less time to reach that first milestone. But if you never start, you may never reach it.

One key aspect of the 401K plan is that it can be taken out of your paycheck automatically. It is easier to stay on course with a payroll deduction plan. If you need to choose to do one or the other (401k vs IRA), I suggest contributing the maximum to the 401K first. It comes out before taxes (unless you choose a Roth 401K), so it can reduce your tax burden and make saving a little easier. Plus, if your employer does match all or a portion of your contribution, which many do, your earnings will be much higher.

My former employer matched my contribution up to the first five percent of my salary. That means I was earning a 50 percent return in the first year on each contribution (I contributed 10% through payroll deductions). That can really supercharge your retirement savings plan! Now, I want to add a few more rows to that table and show you how long it takes to reach the next milestone of $50,000. I'll pick up where we left off and repeat year four.

Year	Added/Yr. to IRA	Average Gain	IRA Yr.-end Balance	Added/Yr. to 401K	Average Gain	401K Yr.-end Balance	Total Balance
4	$5,500	$947	$19,980	$3,612	$559	$12,150	$32,130
5	$5,500	$1,399	$26,879	$3,792	$851	$16,793	$43,672
6	$5,500	$1,881	$34,260	$3,982	$1,176	$21,951	$56,211

If we round a little and do the math, we find that it takes only 2.2 years to accumulate the second $25,000 to hit the $50,000 milestone. Notice that it took only 2/3 of the time that the first $25,000 took to accumulate. That is because your money was working for you, and you are contributing a little more to your 401K each year; that is the magic of compound interest. As you will see, the more you accumulate, the more money you earn and the fewer contributions you make as a percentage of the annual gain.

I want to add a few more columns to further illustrate how it works. The assumptions remain the same, but now your savings will literally begin to carry more and more of the load. Once again, I will begin by including the last year from the previous table for continuity.

Year	Added/Yr. to IRA	Average Gain	IRA Yr.-end Balance	Added/Yr. to 401K	Average Gain	401K Yr.-end Balance	Total Balance
6	$5,500	$1,881	$34,260	$3,982	$1,176	$21,951	$56,211
7	$5,500	$2,398	$42,158	$4,181	$1,537	$27,668	$69,827
8	$5,500	$2,951	$50,609	$4,390	$1,937	$33,995	$84,605
9	$5,500	$3,543	$59,652	$4,610	$2,380	$40,985	$100,637

It takes about 3.5 years to accumulate another $50,000 when it required 5.5 years for the first. With the money working harder for you each year, it only takes nine years to accumulate that first $100,000 in savings. It may take ten or twelve, or it may take fewer years depending upon market conditions, your investment selections, and whether or not you had to deal with emergencies and setbacks along the way. However, consistency is the part that you can control, and adding a planned amount every year will eventually get you there.

Notice that in year nine, if you look at the two columns labeled Average Gain and add the two together, your earnings/gain is $5,922, over 58 percent of your total contributions for the year. Your money is beginning to pull its weight, and it gets even better as time passes. The keys to investing are consistency, compounding, and time (patience). Add in selectivity, and you may be able to beat the average returns in the tables. If you do, the milestone achievements will happen faster. I will get into that part of investing in some of the later chapters.

One last look at the progression to get to $200,000 from $100,000. Remember that it took nine years to reach the first hundred grand. Let's see how long the second one takes.

Year	Added/Yr. to IRA	Average Gain	IRA Yr.-end Balance	Added/Yr. to 401K	Average Gain	401K Yr.-end Balance	Total Balance
9	$5,500	$3,543	$59,652	$4,610	$2,380	$40,985	$100,637
10	$5,500	$4,176	$69,328	$4,840	$2,869	$48,694	$118,021
11	$5,500	$4,853	$79,681	$5,082	$3,409	$57,184	$136,865
12	$5,500	$5,578	$90,758	$5,336	$4,003	$66,523	$157,282
13	$5,500	$6,353	$102,611	$5,603	$4,657	$76,783	$179,394
14	$5,500	$7,183	$115,294	$5,883	$5,375	$88,041	$203,335

It only took another five years instead of nine! Now, look at the total annual estimated gains in year 14. We added $11,383 to our savings, but our money earned $12,558, which is 110 percent of the amount saved in the year. By the time we hit $300,000, our money should have increased our balance by 55 percent more than our savings.

Getting to $1 Million

Finally, I want to include another table that summarizes how long, on average, it should take this young man (or woman) who is just starting out in life to reach the $1 million milestone with the approximate number of years it should take to attain each new milestone, adding $100,000 for each interval.

Milestones	1st	2nd	3rd	4th	5th	6th
Yrs. to reach	3.3	2.2	3.5	5	3.5	2.6
Targets	$25,000	$50,000	$100,000	$200,000	$300,000	400,000
Milestones	7th	8th	9th	10th	11th	12th
Yrs. to reach	2.3	2	1.8	1.5	1.4	1.2
Targets	$500,000	$600,000	$700,000	$800,000	$900,000	$1,000,000

Add all the years to reach each milestone from one to the next, from $100,000 to $1 million, and we get an estimated 21.3 years. It takes nine years to reach $100,000 and then another 21.3 to add another $900,000. That adds up to just over 30 years. If you start right out of college, you could be a millionaire by the time you reach 52! Funny how that works out to how old I was when I retired, isn't it?

Unfortunately, I cannot claim to have followed this plan to the letter because I started late, and I really did not comprehend the power of compound interest until later in life. Live and learn. But, if you are reading this book, hopefully, this chapter has burned the importance of compound interest into your brain. It really does work! It is how the average person gets rich and how the rich get richer.

I promised a real-life example, so allow me to use a stock that I have owned and show how compounding works in the real world. Let me make it truly clear, though, that this example does not represent a recommendation to buy this stock at the current price. 3M (ticker: MMM), the maker of Post-it notes, has been paying a dividend without interruption for 100 years and has increased the dividend in each of the last 64 consecutive years. It is a great company and has rewarded investors well in the past, but there are no guarantees it will continue to do as well in the future. But right now, we are looking back. I will explain how I look forward in a later chapter.

One could have bought 3M at year-end 1986 for $116.62 per share. It traded in August of 2021 for a price of about $195.35 years later. That does not sound so great at face value, but there are two factors we need to add to the picture. First, the stock split three times since 1986, so if an investor had bought 100 shares for $116.62 ($11,662) in December 1986 and had held them the entire time, s/he would now own 800 shares valued at $156,280. It is starting to sound surprisingly good now, isn't it? But wait – there is more!

We need to include the dividends that have been paid over the last 35 years by the company. If you just collected all those dividends and did nothing with them, you would have another $38,862 on top of the appreciation for a total of $195,142. You would have received $4,736 in dividends just in 2021 alone.

That works out to a yield on the original investment of over 40 percent!

Now, if you had reinvested all those dividends at the time of receipt, you would have even more shares, and you would be collecting even more dividends every year. You would own about 1,411 shares instead of 800, and you would have about $275,639 of stock. All from one initial investment of $11,662, from reinvesting the dividends and 35 years of patience. 3M is not the best company to invest in over that period; I could have chosen many companies that have performed far better. I just wanted to select a good, solid company that most people would recognize.

That is the true power of compound interest, the eighth wonder of the world!

Quality, compounding, patience, consistency, and a solid plan are the foundation of building wealth. Amazing things are possible for even those with average jobs if they stick to the plan. Let us look at a real-life example of a woman with an average job who left behind over $18 million when she departed this life.

Interlude 1

The Secretary[6]

Gladys Holm died at the age of 86 in 1997. She was a retired secretary who never earned more than $15,000 a year in her life. She had never married and lived alone in a small apartment in Evanston, Indiana, during her working years.

During her retirement, she gave stuffed animals to children at Children's Memorial Hospital in Chicago. She was known as the "Teddy Bear Lady." She had witnessed the hospital saving a little girl who was special to Ms. Holm many years earlier. She never forgot. When she died, her will designated an $18 million gift to the hospital.

But that's not all she did. While she was giving the children the stuffed animals, it allowed her to get to know the families. Whenever she learned that one of those families was experiencing financial difficulties due to the medical bills piling up, she quietly took care of the problem.

To be honest, she was lucky. But she made her luck. She was a secretary to the founder of a company, American Hospital Supply Company. When the company went public, she was given stock options, converted them into stock, and held onto them. She also bought other stocks, mostly in healthcare, and held onto those as well, using dividends collected from her ever-growing portfolio.

Nobody knew she had any money. Even her niece, the little girl who was saved by the hospital, had no clue. She did not live ostentatiously, but she lived the life she chose and was very comfortable. The point is that she worked hard and was rewarded, then bought stock in high-quality companies that she understood and held onto throughout her life. Time and compound interest did the rest.

---

[6] https://www.nytimes.com/1997/08/03/us/teddy-bear-lady-gave-her-heart-plus-18-million.html. My rendition of her story is an abbreviated summary of the original story.

Part II:
Asset Allocation

Chapter 4:
Allocation Across Multiple Assets

Why Diversify

I mentioned the different asset classes I would discuss in the introduction: stocks, bonds, real estate, and precious metals. Why is it supposed to be smart to distribute your investments across multiple asset types? The answer is diversification to reduce risk. If all your investments are in one asset class (such as stocks) and that asset class falls broadly, then you have nothing but losses. But, if you invest in multiple asset classes, the thinking is that some assets will rise as others will fall, providing a counterweight, more balance, and less overall risk. It makes sense in principle, but in practice, it does not always work out as planned.

When the Federal Reserve Bank (or U.S. central bank which manages the nation's currency) raises interest rates to fight inflation, bond prices fall (because the price of a bond moves in the opposite direction of its yield). A rising interest rate environment also causes headwinds for stocks and real estate because the cost of capital increases. The economy slows down, resulting in reduced demand for commodities, therefore pulling most commodity prices lower. Some assets will fall more, and some will fall less, but overall, most assets will fall in value at the same time. Some will fall more and earlier than others, while some will begin to recover well ahead of others. Diversification does reduce risk, but it does not eliminate risk.

So, I take a different approach. Since I try to buy only when an asset (whether it be a stock, bond, rental property, or commodity) has become a bargain, I can afford to hold it for the long term. I prefer to buy assets that provide regular income in the form of dividends, interest, or rent. The income enables me to hold on for the long term while continuing to collect the income. I prefer to invest in a manner that generates layer upon layer of income that rises regularly over time. The regular income (in the form of cash) piles up while I wait for the next bargain to appear.

I do not try to maintain any special weighting across my asset classes. Instead, I just buy whatever asset class becomes cheap relative to its intrinsic value and provides a minimum level of income yield. So, I tend to create diversification within my portfolio over time, not all at once. Otherwise, I would end up paying too much to keep my portfolio balanced by overpaying for one or the other type of asset when its price was not a bargain.

It has been my experience that if you concentrate on finding bargains across the spectrum of asset classes, you will eventually become as diversified as needed with a much lower overall cost basis (price paid). Also, if you concentrate on buying assets that provide consistently rising income, you will be more likely to have cash available when more bargain opportunities become available. Again, it gets easier as time goes by, and you accumulate more assets in your portfolio, most of which provide rising, recurring income. You may ask how income from bonds can rise. Honestly, they do not. However, you can reinvest the income regularly, either in more bonds or other income-producing assets. Then, taken together, your portfolio income keeps rising every year, providing more capital (cash) to reinvest.

Chapter 5:
Allocations to Cash, When and Why

A frequently asked question that people often ask is: "Which assets present the best value when I have the cash to invest?" This gets to the meat of my investing philosophy because of the implied timing inherent to the question. Usually, when an investor has built up cash, s/he wants to put that cash to work as soon as possible, and they should. But there are two ways to do so (probably many more, but I have my favorites). First, if there are no bargains to be had at the time, I tend to sit in cash and wait patiently for one or another prospective investment to fall into a range that I consider to offer a good long-term value. Yes. This sounds like value investing, and it is, but with a slight twist. The investing style label is generally used to describe a systematic method of investing in stocks. We need to broaden that perception! When we do, it opens up all types of opportunities that mere stock investors completely miss.

First, I need to explain what I do with my cash while I wait for opportunities. Right now, we receive 5% interest on our checking accounts at our credit union (much better than what banks offer). We are limited to one account per person, so my wife and I each have a separate account. We are also limited to earning that rate on a maximum of $25,000 per account. We keep a little more than the maximum in each account to earn the maximum interest. So, that means we have a little more than $50,000 in cash sitting in checking.

As far as the rest of our cash holdings, both emergency cushion and cash waiting to be invested, I have two options to consider.

We also invest some in either short-term (6-12 months) CDs (Certificates of Deposit) with our credit union or in short-term Treasury Bills using TreasuryDirect.com. We do this whenever we can earn more on our excess cash than with my second option and when the Federal Reserve is not holding the overnight Fed Funds rate near zero. Another option for when short-term interest rates are elevated is iShares Short Treasury Bond ETF (SHV), which has extremely low risk to principal and yields somewhere between the 1-year and 2-year rates. Alternatively, an even better yield can be obtained from the SPDR Bloomberg 1–3-month T-Bill ETF (BIL) if the short-term rates are higher than the 1-year rate.

When interest rates get higher and appear to be near the top (meaning the Federal Reserve has stopped raising interest rates or is beginning to lower rates), I tend to buy Vanguard GNMA (Symbol: VFIIX) Fund shares. The reason is simple: During the crash of 2008, VFIIX went up while stocks and most other assets went down in value. However, this strategy only works when I expect interest rates to fall (meaning the economy is entering a recession, and the Federal Reserve is more likely to lower rates). If interest rates are already low and I expect rates to rise (especially when the Fed wants to fight inflation), I stay clear of VFIIX because rising rates will lower the value of its holdings (mortgages act like bonds, which move inversely in price when yields change). That means the Net Present Value of assets it holds will fall in value, yields will drop, and investors will sell, putting pressure on the share price to fall as well. This is not a buy-and-hold forever investment vehicle, but it can be a good holding in the right interest-rate environment. Not only do I receive a decent yield, but there is good appreciation potential, as well.

The same principles apply to mortgage R.E.I.T.s (real estate investment trusts). When interest rates are high and more likely to fall than rise, I tend to buy Annaly Capital Management (NLY) to collect a high dividend while I wait for the price of the stock to rise. But when interest rates are low and more likely to rise than fall, I stay away from NLY.

If the Fed Funds rate is near zero, there are no real alternatives to letting the cash sit in a money market account, earning next to nothing without taking unnecessary risks.

Chapter 6:
Finding Buying Opportunities in Stocks

The sort of opportunity I wait for in stocks can come in two different forms: a crash creating long-term value bargains in quality companies or an increase in economic growth. Stagnate economic growth when the markets are making new all-time highs does not usually lead to another long bull market.

Having said that, there are often great long-term opportunities available most of the time when a company or industry is out of favor by Wall Street analysts. We just need to do our due diligence to make sure these represent real opportunities and not real problems that cannot be overcome. As I finalize this book (mid-2025), the stock market is making new highs, but there are still many bargains for dividend investors because much of the advance has come from just a handful of very large companies. The broader market of stocks has lagged, presenting some good opportunities to buy industry leaders that are paying more than 3% dividend yields (some yielding 5% or more). As I write this, Annaly Capital Management is yielding ~13%. Interest rates have probably peaked, and most economists are expecting the Fed to begin cutting interest rates soon. You know where a good portion of my cash is sitting right now! This is not a recommendation. Just letting readers know what I am doing at the moment. By the time you read this, things may have changed.

Here are some examples of identifying bargains: Back in mid-2009, the stock market signaled that the bear was ready to go back into hibernation and that stocks were on sale. Value investors had a plethora of quality companies' stocks to pick from. But housing values were still falling. Precious metals prices had dropped like rocks (pun intended) only to soar to new extreme highs on the fear of inflation.

Municipal bond prices fell and created excellent value for quality issues well into 2010, providing federal tax-free yields of more than five percent. Treasury bonds gave investors quite a ride up in 2008, then down into early 2009 as the Financial Crisis unfolded, then back up into 2010 as investors continued to seek safety, only to fall again into January 2011 as the economy stalled temporarily. However, from that point until the Federal Reserve began raising interest rates again, Treasuries were a great asset class to hold for appreciation. But the yields were anemic, so Treasuries did not make the cut for me.

Each asset class offered great value at one or more points during the crisis and the aftermath. As an investor, I began buying stocks slowly at first because I was not certain at the time regarding inflation (too much of which can kill a bull market move in stocks).

I realized that the "all clear" sign to buy stock was signaled loud and clear when the Fed announced Operation Twist. That announcement told me that the Fed was not going to quit until it had created a recovery in the U.S. economy. That was also about the time that I understood that inflation was not the problem, but rather the battle waged by the Fed and central banks around the world would be to ward off deflation. Connecting the dots brought me to the understanding that the Fed and its global brethren would be fighting deflation by trying to create inflation (unsuccessfully), and the result would be rising asset prices. I was a little late to the party but still got some great bargains beginning in 2010.

Had I just believed the indicators I followed, I would have been buying stocks much sooner. Oh, well. Here are the two rules I try to follow to determine when a bottom for stocks is in. But I felt it necessary to err on the side of caution due to my initial uncertainty about the inflation/deflation debate. These indicators, when taken together, can be used for either an individual stock, an index, or an ETF (exchange-traded fund).

Indicator Number 1

If the market exhibits a day of capitulation with a relatively strong reversal at the close, it is often a good sign of a significant bottom. This is difficult to identify correctly at the moment because emotions are running wild, and there is a fear that things could get even worse. The best way to describe this is that the daily action looks like a flash crash, falling five percent or more from the prior day's close as intraday buying closes the session flat or higher.

While this indicator can often work in identifying a bottom, it can also show some false positives. That means that it appears to be at bottom, but within a few days, the downward trend continues. In other words, it is not always reliable. But when the market drops that much intraday and reverses, it is usually a good time to start to add some small positions that you want to hold for the long term, especially if the market is already down more than 20 percent overall from its 52-week high. The uncertainty of this one indicator on its own means I need a second indicator to corroborate the first.

That brings me to…

Indicator Number 2

This one is straightforward, and I have found it to be far more reliable. The price of the underlying stock (or index) must rise above the 200-day SMA (Simple Moving Average), and the 50-day SMA must rise above the 200-day SMA. I have found that when that occurs, the bottom for the index and/or stock is usually made. By employing this rule, we will miss some of the potential gains off the bottom, but we can rest assured that the bottom is either in or very nearly so. Sometimes, a market index will fall again for an abbreviated period, but it eventually starts to rise again within a few months at most.

While there is no one foolproof method of determining that a bottom has been made, this one has proven to be the best. One could get a false positive reading from a short bear market rally, but only if it lasts long enough (usually more than 2 months) because of the 200-day SMA, which takes time to reverse course. However, such rallies rarely last more than two months, which is required for that to happen.

The point of all this is that it is not so much "when" you have the cash available that is important as it is to have cash available when an asset class becomes a bargain. I always try to accumulate cash for when I need it, especially when most of the assets I would like to own have become expensive.

How I allocate between asset classes comes down to an overall approach of deciding which class of assets is most likely to offer the best long-term value and help me achieve my long-term income goals. I may sell a rental property or two when I think housing prices have gotten out of hand. Those lead to long-term capital gains, so the taxes are not so bad. However, the decision on such sales is made based on regional valuations, not national ones, for real estate. The one I have left from the 2009 purchases is in Indiana, where housing prices are still lower than the national average and have not risen as much. It may be time to let that one go soon, too.

My income from real estate rentals should continue to rise over time (or at least remain steady) without much downside risk because of where I own my properties. That has not always been the case in my lifetime. I learned a valuable lesson about investing in real estate in Texas during the mid-1980s. I was underwater on that one for several years but finally got out with a significant gain in 2001, just before I retired. I did much better on Colorado and Virginia properties. WHEN I bought those properties was more important than any other factor. Bargains!

My asset allocation between asset classes varies over time. I add an asset when it appears to meet my criteria for providing a long-term, rising stream of income beginning at a level that I consider a bargain. It is not so much a matter of holding X% of this asset or Y% of that asset for me. I just want to invest in any asset when, and only when, I can get great value for my money. Otherwise, I will hold onto my cash and just wait until another bargain arises.

Summing Up

Stocks and stock funds are my largest holding, accounting for more than 50 percent of my investments; cash is currently second, accounting for about 22 percent; real estate is third, accounting for about 15 percent; bonds and bond funds account for about 10 percent of my holdings; and precious metals account for about three percent of the total.

There is no magic number for me. I add to any asset class when it is cheap compared to its historical norms and can provide better long-term income than any other class. How long have I been doing it this way? I finally figured out that this is what I should be doing shortly after I retired. I was lucky to have done well before that without a defined plan. This is where I must insert that "I wish I had known at 25 what I know now!" All I did prior to that was save as much as I could and invest in what I thought could provide an above-average return. I guessed right often enough to make it work, but there were some very painful setbacks. Now, I focus on quality and income, letting total return take care of itself. I also do my best to avoid significant losses. I hope my experiences can help others avoid some, if not all, of the mistakes I made.

Chapter 7:
Allocating Bonds

This is one area where I wish I had known while younger what I do now in a big way. When I was younger, bond investing seemed too boring. Seven percent? No, thank you, I thought. But that sure looks good now! So, what I intend to do here, especially for the benefit of those who are early in their investing lives, is to start out by explaining what I have done and then end up by explaining what I wish I had done (or would have done differently) or should have done and why.

The first time I seriously considered buying bonds was in 1980, when 30-year Treasuries yielded over 12 percent. I did not realize at the time just how good 12 percent was. I was young, 30 years old, and had a great job making more money (in real, inflation-adjusted terms) than I would again for nearly 20 years. I passed on that one to my own detriment. Those yields made me think, though, and then about a year later, when 30-year Treasuries hit fifteen percent, I considered it again. This time, I had left a great job (probably another blunder, but I survived) and was concerned about tying up too much of my savings because I was in transition. I was worried that I might need the money and did not understand the whole concept of how the price of bonds goes up as the yield falls. If that had clicked for me, then I believe I would have bought the bonds and hoped for lower rates. Of course, that would have been a terrific investment.

I did not give bonds another thought until I read something about the zero-coupon Treasury bonds, called CATS, and calculated how much they could be worth over time. The first ten years were interesting, the next ten got downright impressive, and from there on out, it was heaven. This all went through my mind two years later, but by that time, I had bought my first condo to live in and used most of what I had saved to live on for the down payment. I had left my great job in the middle of a recession and moved. Finding good employment was tough.

If you recall my story from earlier, I told my friends about the CATS bonds to save for college. By putting the bonds in the name of their child, my friends avoided some of the tax consequences, but not all. As the story goes, they locked in 12 percent for 30 years. I did not. They were happy. I was sad (and I am still sad to this day).

Finally, as I retired in 2002, I began to realize how important the secure income stream would be and decided to buy municipal bonds. I stuck with quality, only buying A-rated Muni bonds, and only bought when I could find a yield above 4.8 percent. I did not find much that met my requirements very often, but when 2010 rolled around, I filled my quota, and I am glad I did. The yield still did not look that great after the level of rates I had experienced earlier in life, but it does now, and I am glad I took the plunge when I did. I like the fact that my wife and I have not paid federal income tax on our bond interest income. And, no, the AMT does not affect me. I keep my income down to what I need in taxable accounts and let it build in my tax-deferred accounts. So far, that has worked out.

Now, if I had it all to do over again, I would have bought those 30-year Treasuries with at least half of my savings when the yield was over 12 percent. And when those bonds would have matured, I would have looked for more with which to replace them. A five percent fully taxable yield has never looked that good to me, so I would have laddered the maturities, accepting a lower yield in return for having more cash available to reinvest should a better opportunity occur. It is like another way to store cash for future investing while still getting a yield. Also, with shorter maturities, there is less risk to the principal amount, so selling those bonds is an option should a great investment opportunity window open before maturity.

Maybe I should hold more bonds in my portfolio for the sake of diversification, but outside of tax-free Muni bonds, I do not see the point of investing in long-term bonds, Treasuries, or corporate bonds when rates are low. That puts too much principal at risk at a rate with which I cannot live (4.5% or less). The interest earned in a taxable account is taxable as regular income, so I would not get to keep the full amount.

There will come a time when rates rise to 7 percent or more on Treasuries and highly rated corporate bonds. Maybe next time, I will be able to pull the trigger. I think it gets easier to buy bonds the older I get. My plan is to move more to bonds in the future when those rates get up to a level I can accept. Live and learn.

Chapter 8:
Allocating Real Estate

Well, I learned some tough lessons in this area. The biggest one is probably that you really need to know the area in which you are investing. The next one is that it is best to invest in cities that have a diverse economic foundation, with the leading employers likely to continue to grow at a sustainable, reasonable rate over time. I like college towns that are also state capitals but have several other industries that contribute as much or more to the local employment and economy as the college or state. I do not like a city that is dominated by just one or a few large employers. I do not like cities that go through booms and busts. I like steady as she goes local economies and cities that I feel I can depend on for decades to come. I also do not like large cities. That is just a personal thing, as I would not want to live near my rental properties. It is not a prerequisite to live near rental properties, but it does help a lot. So, I also do not want to own properties where I would not feel safe or want to live for any reason. I like to feel connected to what I own.

I did not start out understanding any of that. I had to learn it all the hard way, trying to understand why I was successful on one set of properties and why I failed (or did not get the return I expected) on others. I think that if I was young and just starting out investing, even now, I would commit more of my portfolio to real estate. But I would be much more systematic about it than I have been. My first property was a condominium I lived in in Austin, Texas. I bought it in 1982. Mortgage rates were 16.5 percent. I bought it with a mortgage that had the rate "bought down" to 8.5 percent. So, in the beginning, everything seemed great. But then I got married, we moved, and I turned the condominium into a rental because the real estate market was soft. I assumed that real estate would get better. It did not for quite a long time. That one became what those in the real estate business call an alligator. It just ate me alive for a while. I finally got a new mortgage at a lower rate, and the cash flow turned positive. Over the total holding period, I did have a positive total return, but it was nothing to write home about.

The second property was the first one that my wife and I bought together, a fourplex. By this time, I was a little gun-shy and, being a veteran, used my G.I. Bill benefit to buy it with no down payment. We received cash at closing because I arranged to close early in the month and receive most of the current month's rent. The rent covered the closing costs for us with a little money to spare. We moved into one of the units and lived rent-free because the rent from the other three units covered the mortgage payment. The rents have increased a little every year, averaging about 3 percent. A local manager takes care of the property, but I have always made all the decisions about maintenance and paid all the bills directly. Taking an active role in managing the properties is imperative for tax reasons. The mortgage is fully paid off as of a few years ago. There are now four rental checks coming in every month.

I found that rental properties in Lincoln, Nebraska, were a good investment for the long term. While the University of Nebraska seems to dominate downtown on football Saturdays, the city meets all of my criteria. Nebraska, and especially Lincoln, hardly noticed the Great Recession in terms of unemployment. That makes for a steady real estate market. My goal in real estate is not focused on appreciation, as one might expect. Instead, I want my properties to provide positive cash flow from day one so that the mortgage gets paid for me. Sometimes, it requires a lot of patience to wait for the right property with the right cash flow prospects to become available. But when it does, it is worth the wait. Remember that when you buy a property for $100,000 (hypothetically, to make the math easy), you only put 20 percent down. The cash flow is on your investment of $20,000, not the full value of the property. If you only start out with a $100 monthly positive cash flow, and that amounts to less than 20 percent of the rent collected, the annual increases can be substantial. Let us take a hypothetical example and keep the numbers easy to follow.

Purchase price: $100,000. Monthly rent: $860

Mortgage payment (including escrow for taxes and insurance): $550

Water & Sewer: $30

Maintenance & Repairs: $120

Management fees: $60 (usually 7% of rents)

That leaves $100 per month in cash flow. The percentages are based upon actual prices and rents that can come available in Lincoln, a 5 percent mortgage over 30 years, 20 percent down payment, and 7 percent management fees. Your income is $1,200 per year, or 6 percent of your initial investment during the first year. Now, let us assume that you raise the rent by 3 percent per year. That means rent will go to $885 per month. Maintenance and management will rise along with water, sewer, taxes, and insurance. Your expenses should increase at about the same pace as rents, if not a little slower. So, the expenses increase by $10 per month, and your cash flow increases by $15. That is a 15 percent increase in cash flow. Now, your return (yield) in year 2 is almost 7 percent on your initial investment. So, it continues, and by year 20, your free cash flow will be $500 per month. In year 30, the mortgage is paid off, and your monthly income is about $1,200 per month ($14,400 per year), which is still rising. All that is done with an initial investment of $20,000. I should remind you again that this is hypothetical, but over the long term, it really can work out this way. That 4-plex I bought in the late 1980s for $100,000 is now worth more than triple that and provides a steady stream of income.

It never goes quite that smoothly, especially if you do not put aside money for maintenance and repairs, whether there are expenses or not. That, to me, is one of the keys because if you accumulate funds for future repairs before those repairs become necessary, everything works out much better. You may go into the hole on maintenance at times, and how much needs to be set aside each month varies depending on the age and condition of each property. I prefer to make certain, through inspections before purchase, that there are no significant deferred maintenance issues.

Never get emotional about a property. Be rational and be ready to walk away if there are problems. There will always be another opportunity if you are patient. I know - easier said than done.

Real estate investing takes time and effort, but it is something that most people can learn to understand and do well over a lifetime.

Chapter 9:
Allocating Precious Metals

I will not spend much ink on this topic because it is not necessary to invest in gold or silver. It is merely a personal preference, and an investor can do fine without it. Many folks get more paranoid as they age. That is not necessarily a terrible thing. Caution is good. However, committing too much to an asset that does not pay any interest or provide an income of any kind can be superfluous.

I started with a coin collection when I was a teen. I have kept much of it. I bought a few bags of junk silver coins during the financial crisis. I guess I got caught up in the emotion and a little bit of the survival idea should the worst happen. I do not expect to ever need those coins for anything. At some point in the future, inflation will again rear its ugly head, and I will be happy to have something that is going up in value. I plan to hold on to the coins but not add more to my small stash.

The idea that gold and silver hold their value over the long term does not make complete sense. The price of gold goes up and down relative to the value of a dollar. It does not generate any income, so an investor is totally reliant on the accumulated appreciation. Below are a couple of charts that illustrate why I prefer stocks over precious metals.

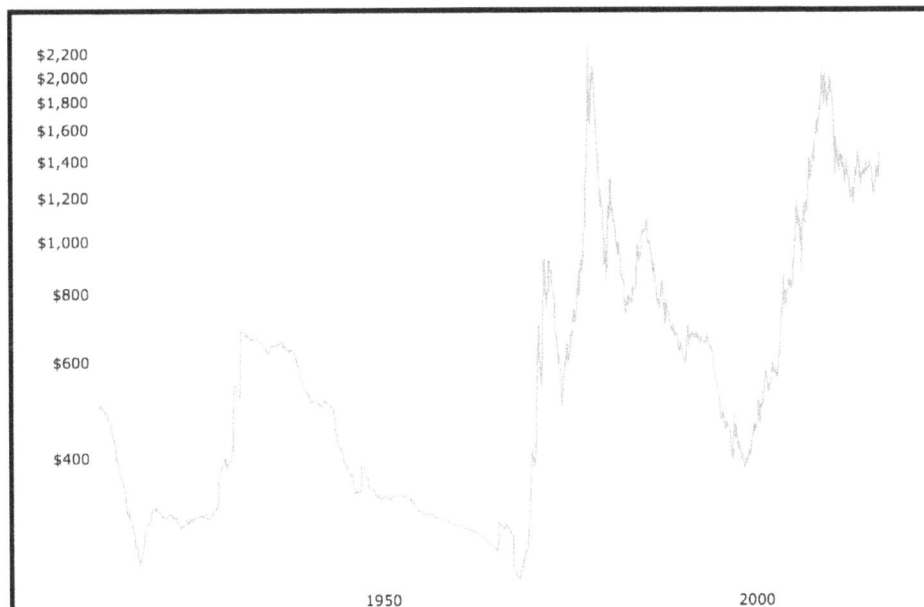

The chart above shows the price of gold versus the U.S. dollar over the past 100 years. Yes, you would have made money holding gold over this entire period, but what if you had bought gold during the 1980s and wanted to retire in 2000? You would have lost over half of your investment.

Now, let us look at how gold has done compared to the stock market indices.

Stocks vs. Gold and Silver

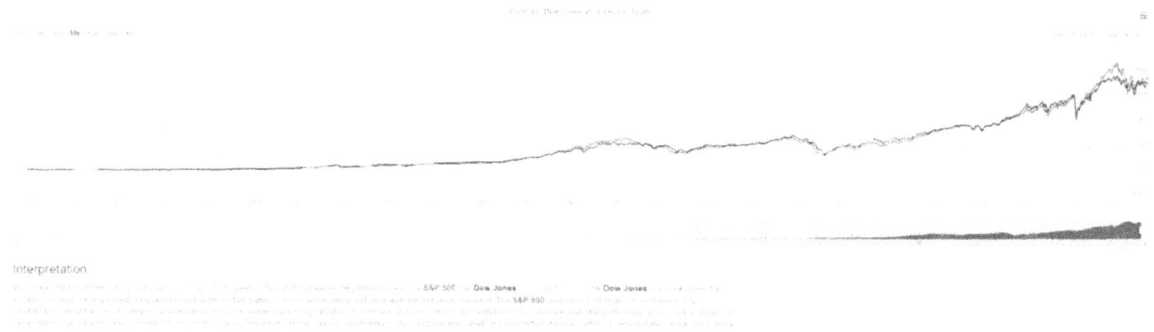

Interpretation

As you can see, gold has underperformed stocks for most of the last 126 years. Both the S&P 500 and the Dow Jones industrial averages have provided much higher and more consistent returns, especially since the Financial Crisis of 2007-09. Of course, gold has made significant gains since 2022, but I would refer you back to the first of these two charts to understand that the price of gold can be extremely volatile. That does not equate to "holding value" in my book.

If the fiat currency regime fails at some point (I am not predicting that it will), my meager stash of silver coins could be easy to use for buying small items. However, if that happened, I think I'd rather own a warehouse full of toilet paper for bartering purposes.

Chapter 10:
The Asset that Always Goes Up in Value When All Others Go Down

The hardest lesson I have ever learned

Growing up as a teenager in the 1960s, I had to listen to my dad complain about inflation... a lot. Everything was getting more expensive, and he owned his own business. Raising the prices he charged his customers was difficult for him, but he had to do it because the cost of everything he used in his business - a small resort on the Canadian border waters of Minnesota - was rising. He kept telling me that the value of the dollar was going down. That lesson stuck with me.

As I got a little older, I went off to college after spending two glorious, all-expense paid, year-long vacations in southeast Asia, courtesy of my Uncle Sam. Yes, sir, I got to spend time hiking trails and communing with nature, with plenty of activities to keep my adrenaline flowing. What a rush! But being in a reconnaissance unit in Vietnam or recovering helicopters that had been shot down wasn't always as fun as the recruiting sergeant made it out to be.

While in college, I took a full load of classes and worked full-time to pay my own way, helped once again by my good old Uncle, who sent me 36 monthly checks to help with the cost of college. Every time I noticed that my savings had burgeoned to over $2,000 (I do not know why that number triggered an urge, but it did), I had to buy something. Otherwise, inflation would just eat away at that money as it became worth a little less each year. Thanks, Dad! Actually, I should not blame him because he taught me how to save. He just stopped with that lesson and the one about inflation. The spending thing I came up with on my own.

Then came my first professional job, with a company car, a liberal expense account, great pay, a stock bonus, and profit sharing. It was a nice start right out of college. This time, I was so busy that my savings piled up faster than I could spend it. This was back in the late 1970s, and interest rates were rising. At that point, I knew nothing about stocks and nothing about real estate. I had no interest in bonds - something that I now really wish I had understood well back then. By 1980, I had saved $25,000. That does not sound like much today, but in 1980, it seemed like a small fortune to me. If I had understood how bonds worked then, I would have used all of it to buy 30-year U.S. Treasuries.

I must admit right now that I did nothing very well with those savings. I could explain, but none of it would be very instructive or beneficial to understand. To summarize, I left that good job and, for a good while after, did not have the same level of income, but I did not adjust how I lived. While this is not the lesson of the article, it was a good one to learn early in life. Eventually, the money began to run low, and I was forced to change some spending habits. Life would have been better if I had made the necessary adjustments earlier. Once again, live and learn.

Looking back, something that did not sink in at the time but has since become clear is that when interest rates are extremely high and housing values fall, it is a good time to buy real estate. Interest rates will eventually drop, providing an opportunity to refinance, resulting in lower mortgage payments. Falling interest rates also tend to help boost real estate values at a higher rate than average. But that is not the lesson of this section either.

The lesson that was so hard to learn was to unlearn what I learned from my dad and from many other sources: holding cash without receiving any interest or income is a sure way for your savings to lose value because of inflation. I learned that not earning more than inflation on my money would cause me to permanently lose buying power. That is what I was taught all my life. The hard part was to learn that what I had learned was wrong!

Am I losing you? Stick with me a little longer, and you will understand that what I am saying is true. It is not what any financial institution wants you to understand. Having money sitting in an account that may not keep up with inflation seems ridiculous, doesn't it? That is what we keep hearing. But that way of thinking just gets people to invest when they should be on the sidelines waiting for a better opportunity. Wall Street cannot make a profit on your money if you let it just sit there. They need to earn a small percentage to manage your assets!

Cash is the one asset class that goes up in value when all other assets go down. Think about it for a few moments.

If you have $10,000 in cash that you could invest in the stock of a great company at $50 with a dividend of $1.25 now, would you do better than holding the cash until the share price went down to $40 two years later with a dividend of $1.40? The answer should be obvious. But rather than looking at a hypothetical situation, I want to offer two real examples from my own portfolio.

I decided back around the beginning of 1997 that I wanted to own shares of PepsiCo (symbol: PEP). My reason for liking PEP so much was that I was drinking several cans of the stuff every day at work. Most people drink coffee for the caffeine. I drank soda, and my favorite was Pepsi. I know that is not a great reason, but I was just starting out. Besides, I knew I was not the only one who liked Pepsi products. After studying the stock, I had some regret for not having bought it earlier and decided that I would only buy it if the price dropped back to $33 per share again. All of 1997 went by, and the price did little other than rise. It was a little different over most of 1998. I almost gave up and bought the stock in March of 1998 at around $40. But at that price, the dividend yield was under one percent. I decided to wait.

Finally, sometime in late summer, I learned about good-until-canceled buy orders. So, I placed an order to buy some shares at $33 per share, good until canceled, and stopped worrying about it. In early October, the shares traded down below $30, and I got my order filled. I ended up buying the shares at $33. I could have done better, but I reminded myself that I was doing better than if I had bought it at $40. It helped. I have since made another purchase of PEP and will go through that example in a minute.

Now, I want to show you how I did by using an illustration I first wrote about in an article in 2015 and the difference in results between my actual purchase and what would have happened had I pulled the trigger earlier at $40. To keep the math simple, I will assume in both this and the next example that I had $10,000 to invest each time. If I had invested in PEP at $40 per share in March 1998, I would have gotten 250 shares. I would have collected a couple more dividend payments, but the total of dividends I would have collected from then to (June 2015) would be $5,814. My total gain would be $13,617. My original $10,000 investment would be worth $29,431, and my dividend (as indicated) in 2015 would be $680 for a 6.8 percent yield on my original investment. That all sounds good. Today (March 2024), the total annual dividend on those 250 shares is $1,265, or a yield of nearly 13% on my original investment.

Here are the results of the type of return I got by waiting for the price I wanted compared to the above example in table form.

Date	Price	Shares	Total Div.	Gain	Orig. Value	Current Value	2024 Div.	Yld
03/98	$40	250	$14,352	$33,750	$10,000	$43,750	$1265	12.6%
10/98	$33	303	$17,304	$43,025	$10,000	$53,025	$1533	15.3%

The column labeled "Yld" represents the annual yield now earned in the current year on the original investment. Next, I want to look at what I did later in life after learning more about how the value of cash increases when other assets go down. But first, a little rant.

I get tired of hearing that it does not matter if an investor buys shares in a company at the peak of a bull market or at the bottom of a bear market as long as they hold those shares long enough. The difference will become less over time, we are always told, and will eventually become inconsequential. The problem with the examples they use to explain the difference is that they usually assume that the investor buys the same number of shares in both instances. Such examples do not consider the reality that an investor will be able to buy more shares at a lower price with the same amount of cash. Those additional shares result in more gain and a higher dividend yield, and the difference increases over time, especially if one reinvests the dividends each year (something I did not do in the example above; the results would have been better and the difference larger).

If I had followed the conventional wisdom that says it does not matter when you buy and invested $10,000 in PEP shares two months before the stock hit its high in 2007, I would have bought 142 shares at about $69.96, the average price on September 1, 2007. The stock traded as high as $77.41 in November 2007, so I am not taking the top of the market. I actually made a purchase on June 1, 2009, almost two years later. I missed all the dividend income that would have been collected for those two years, but I am glad I did. Check out the results from the date of purchase through 2015 in the chart below. This is only over about eight years. Imagine the difference over a lifetime of investing of 40 years or more.

Date	Price	Shares	Total Div.	Total Gains	Original Value	Value in 2015	Comp Anl Rtn	2015 Div.	Yld
9/1/07	$69.96	142	$2,358	$3,480	$10,000	$15,772	5.9%	$386	3.9%
6/1/09	$52.82	189	$2,467	$7,872	$10,000	$20,339	9.3%	$514	5.1%

The results are obvious. Waiting for a better buying opportunity allowed me to buy more shares, collect more dividends, lock in a much higher yield, and create a superior compound annual return. Again, the returns do not include reinvested dividends or any income on the cash accumulated from collecting those dividends; doing so would only make the comparison more lopsided.

Each time we go through another cycle, I try to get better at identifying when an asset, such as equities, no longer offers me a bargain. At that point, I stop buying and just begin to accumulate until the next time we experience a significant economic recession.

I provided the two examples of my purchases of PEP shares for a reason. The first example, in 1998, represented a modest bear market swoon. The second example, in 2007-2009, was a much more severe recessionary period. The point of the two examples was that it can be beneficial to wait, whether the bear market is deep or relatively small.

Summary

The main point that I hope I have made clear is that when stocks, or any other assets, fall significantly in value, the amount of that asset an investor can purchase with the same amount of cash increases.

Stated differently, when the value of other assets falls, the relative value of cash increases. We need to stop thinking in terms of inflation eating away at the value of our cash and begin thinking in terms of how much more of an asset the same cash today will buy when the value of that asset drops. Cash has value, not only in terms of the everyday items that we buy. As an investment, we need to think of cash as increasing or decreasing in value relative to other assets.

This does not mean that we should only buy at the bottom after an asset class has crashed. What it does mean is that buying quality assets that are deeply undervalued will provide better returns than buying when those assets are overvalued. After a crash like the one we experienced in 2008-09, real estate and equities remained deeply undervalued for several years. There were bargains everywhere I looked. I did not have enough cash to take advantage of all the opportunities. But I had more than most. And I benefited from my patience. Do not expect to be perfect. Just try to do better through each cycle. A lifetime of investing will contain at least 6 to as many as 10 cycles over 40 years.

Chapter 11:
How I Manage My Portfolio

This should be a good place for me to explain how I group my assets. I have four buckets: three buckets consisting of liquid assets like stocks, bonds, options, and cash; one bucket for illiquid assets like real estate held as rental property.

My three buckets of liquid assets consist of one bucket holding stocks, bonds, and a small position in precious metals that I intend to hold for the long term; a bucket holding cash accumulated from dividends, interest, and sales of assets that no longer have reasonable long-term value; and a trading bucket holding short-term investments, hedge positions, and options. Sometimes, a short-term investment can turn into a long-term holding if the growth potential is sustainable.

My long-term holdings consist of dividend-paying stocks, individual bonds or bond funds, and a bag of old, worn silver coins. My reasoning for holding just junk coins is because of the small denominations. I hold precious metals just in case everything goes haywire. If I want to buy stuff during an economic meltdown, I do not want bullion, especially gold, because nobody will want to make change, and I do not want to pay $500 for a few rolls of toilet paper.

The third bucket of my portfolio, or the trading bucket, amounts to no more than ten percent of my overall portfolio and is used primarily to either enhance overall return through growth using riskier stocks with good upside potential or by using options to enhance income. When I buy a "so-called" risky stock, I mean one that does not pay dividends and that I do not intend to hold long term. I look for special situations where a company provides a compelling short-term potential appreciation opportunity. I may hold it for less than a year. For this reason, my short-term holdings are held in a tax-deferred account. I do not want to pay taxes on short-term gains, which are taxed as regular income.

I also use a self-directed, tax-deferred account for all options trades unless I am using LEAPS (Long-term Equity Appreciation Securities options), expecting the underlying stock to rise in value significantly over the next year. But even so, I include these long-term options in my core portfolio (long-term holdings) rather than in my trading bucket.

Because I sell call options against those LEAPS for income, I hold both in a tax-deferred account because those call options will always be short-term, and both securities need to be held together in the same account. Those "short" option positions provide additional income and protect against short-term corrections in the underlying stock price.

I do not intend to get into the details of options trading because that is beyond the purpose of this book. However, I include a brief description of what goes into my trading buckets so readers can understand that it is used for risky assets. The point of this discussion is to limit the risky portion of your portfolio to no more than ten percent.

Chapter 12:
Allocating Within an Asset Class

The purpose of allocating across an asset class is to reduce risk through diversification. If an investor concentrates too much of their portfolio in any one asset or category within the asset class, they could find themselves suffering significantly greater losses than if they had spread those investments against several unrelated holdings. The same is true for allocating across multiple asset classes.

While there were very few places to hide during the Financial Crisis (2007-2009), appropriately called the Great Recession, some assets held up better than others. Thus, proper diversification did help reduce losses for some. But even then, there were losses in about everything, and what mattered most was holding onto the assets that rebounded the fastest. That would be bonds, especially Treasuries, commodities (including precious metals), stocks, and finally, real estate. But all rebounded from the depths of the crisis, and this was the most important lesson. Please do not sell when everything seems lost. "Buy when there's blood in the streets, *even if the blood is your own.*" The quote is credited to Baron Rothschild during the 18th century. He made a fortune buying during the panic that followed Napoleon's defeat at Waterloo.

Allocating Stocks

There will be those who will not like my method of allocating stocks (and the other asset classes as well), but this is just how I do it and the logic behind my (seeming to some) madness.

I rarely buy a stock of a foreign company that is not traded on one of the U.S. exchanges, usually as an ADR (American Depository Receipt). One can achieve plenty of international exposure by purchasing multinational companies with operations worldwide, whether headquartered in the U.S. or abroad. If you want exposure to currency fluctuations, it is also included in the results reported by the big multinationals. Think about it. When the U.S. dollar is strengthening, U.S. multinationals are blaming lower earnings on foreign currency translations. Of course, when the dollar was weakening, the earnings added by foreign exchange (FX) were not reported in the headlines, but those earnings were helped significantly.

Some will say that I risk missing enormous potential gains in China and other emerging markets, but I say I am avoiding the outsized risk by not investing directly in companies for which the accounting standards may vary significantly from U.S. generally accepted accounting practices (GAAP). As a CPA for 29 years, I have an adequate understanding of GAAP, and I am aware of the many different accounting standards followed by other countries (and the standards all change over time in each country). I prefer sticking to what I understand best since, even in the U.S., some companies tend to stretch the standards as far as possible to achieve desired results.

Sticking with what you know is another important concept. If you invest in companies that you do not understand, you do not know what the risks are. Keep things simple and within your realm of understanding or let someone else do the investing for you. Especially when starting out, you do not need to invest in individual stocks. Using funds or ETFs (Exchange Traded Funds), especially Index ETFs, works fine as you work toward your initial milestones.

Chapter 13:
My Basic Rules for Investing

I have five basic rules that I try my best to follow when allocating my stock portfolio.

Rule Number 1 - I allow myself no more than ten percent of my total stock portfolio (not the total portfolio, but just that portion allocated to stocks) to be tradable to take advantage of special situations. This keeps me from taking on too much risk in my portfolio. It is better to avoid mistakes than to risk large losses. By keeping most of my holdings invested long-term, I take better advantage of compounding over time.

One purpose that I use these funds for is to purchase hedge positions to protect the rest of my stock portfolio from significant loss. I never use more than two percent in any given year for this purpose. Often, I can keep the total amount used for hedging below one percent. My reasoning is that even if it costs me an average of 1.5 percent per year for five years or a total of 7.5 percent, I prefer paying for the "insurance" than risking a loss of 30 percent or more if a bear market hits. At the same time, I continue to collect my dividends, and since I only buy what I consider to be high-quality stocks with sustainable competitive advantages that increase dividends every year, why would I want to sell? I like the rising income.

Initially, you do not need to worry about hedging because you do not have that much to lose. So, this concept is only a matter of full disclosure on my part. Once you have more than $100,000 in your stock portfolio, you might want to dig deeper into the concept of hedging, especially when the stock market indices are in record territory and flaunt a historically high P/E (price to earnings) ratio.

Occasionally, there is a company that I believe has significant appreciation potential over the short-to-intermediate term. I want to be able to take advantage of such opportunities and will do so, but only from within this small portion of my portfolio. Setting a limit this way keeps me from making too many boneheaded mistakes. I do not buy a stock on the recommendation of anyone else without doing my own due diligence to make sure I understand the potential risks and rewards. I even keep the funds segregated in a separate account and adjust the amount only once a year. It often sits mostly, if not totally, in cash equivalents, waiting for something to intrigue me.

Rule Number 2 - I try to own stocks of companies from at least eight different sectors.

I do this because of sector rotation. It happens all the time, and I prefer to have at least some of my stock positions involved as the respective sectors are leading the market while other sectors are falling behind. Too much concentration in any given sector can cause more pain than is necessary. Just ask anyone who had an overweight position in technology stocks from the end of 2021 to the end of 2022. Many were down by 20 percent or more, and some were down more than 50 percent. Too much concentration, especially after a long bull run, can kill a portfolio (at least temporarily). And it is avoidable with a little diversification.

Rule Number 3 - I only invest in those industries that I can understand.

This does not mean I must be an expert in the industry, but I can decipher the accounting methods used and compare one company to another or against industry averages. In other words, I want to have the confidence that I can identify the best companies in the industry and, even more importantly, identify the worst companies in the industry (to be avoided).

If you are investing in funds or ETFs, it is generally not a good idea to choose those that have performed best over the recent year. Instead, choose those that have performed better than average over the past 10 years or longer. You want consistency, whether investing in individual stocks or in funds.

Rule Number 4 - I only invest long-term in quality, dividend-paying companies with a consistent record of increasing dividends even in the worst of economic times.

This rule does not apply to my tradable account mentioned under rule 1. But it does apply to every other stock that I own. I only want to own stocks of companies that have sustainable competitive advantages, strong balance sheets, a consistent record of raising dividends annually as well as the free cash flow to continue to be an industry leader and continue raising dividends. If you would like to understand more about how I develop my candidate list for further research, please consider reading my article, "The Dividend Investors Guide to Successful Investing," available at SeekingAlpha.com. It is dated (written in 2012), but the principles still make sense.

Rule Number 5 - I do not allow myself to invest more than 20 percent of my stock portfolio in any one sector initially. If the stocks in the sector appreciate faster than my overall portfolio, I will adjust the weight once a year, but only if it exceeds 25 percent at the time of my annual review.

That one is self-explanatory. Everyone has their own limits. These are mine. Yours can be different. But at least put some thought into this one and get comfortable with how much you hold in any one sector. Remember, concentration can lead to excessive risk. Now, as to how I allocate between the sectors and how I weight them. I start with the S&P 500 weighting of sectors since when I measure how I am doing, I use that index to compare against. But this is just a starting place. I then adjust the weights according to my personal preferences and expectations. Below is a table showing the weighting of sectors as of the time of writing this section.

S&P 500 Index Sector Weights

Information Technology	23%
Health Care	15%
Financials	14%
Consumer Discretionary	9%
Industrials	9%
Communication Services	8%
Consumer Staples	8%
Energy	5%
Utilities	3%
Materials	3%
Real Estate	3%

(Source: S&P Dow Jones Industries)

Ever since the Financial Crisis, I have found myself having difficulty investing in banks. No one knows what the real value of assets on those balance sheets should be with certainty. We do not even know what the banks hold for sure. My portfolio weight for financials is less than five percent. I know I missed a great run, but I see another problem coming soon that dwells within this sector, and I would prefer to miss it. Thank you very much.

I am increasing my holdings in the materials sector because the move away from fossil fuels and the drive to expand and monetize AI (artificial intelligence) will result in huge increases in copper demand. I do not treat this sector as a hold-forever investment because it is very cyclical. I prefer a multi-year position but take profits when I sense the sector pricing is too high or the demand cycle is ending.

Since there will always be a recession in the future and stock values are relatively high at present, I am also underweighting the consumer discretionary sector and industrials. My weighting for energy is lower due to the move toward EVs (electric vehicles) and away from fossil fuels. When these sector prices get lower, I will buy more at bargain prices. Remember, think long term. I am overweight in the utility sector because the demand for electricity will be rising for many years due to AI and electrification and because regulated utilities generally pay rising dividends. Likewise, I overweight consumer staples because of the dividends and stable growth.

So, here is my current sector weighting table:

Health Care	18%
Consumer Staples	15%
Information Technology	21%
Utilities	14%
Energy	3%
Communication Services	8%

Industrials	9%
Financials	5%
Consumer Discretionary	4%
Materials	3%

I should point out that I have been accumulating cash since the fall of 2021, so my holdings include a sizable portion of cash or cash equivalent investments. With interest rates higher in 2023, I am holding my cash in the SPDR Bloomberg 1-3 month T-Bill ETF (BIL), yielding over 5% until I can find more bargains in stocks. Also, I do not own real estate stocks because I own rental properties to satisfy that portion of my diversification. However, choosing to own R.E.I.T.s (Real Estate Investment Trusts) is an acceptable method of diversification for a portion of a portfolio.

I will try to explain how I ended up with this allocation, at least in general terms. Consumer Staples and Utilities are regarded as defensive in nature because the products and services offered by companies in those sectors tend to be the ones we buy regardless of the economic climate.

Who is going to do without food, electricity, water, phone service, or toilet paper (unless you live in Cuba)? Fortunately, our stores rarely run out of necessities, and we rarely choose not to buy such items. However, because I hedge, I can partially ignore the inconvenience of shuffling my portfolio to match the "risk-on" or "risk-off" gyrations due to changes in the perceived economic environment. All the adjustments to portfolios are great for Wall Street because they increase trade volume, which increases its revenue, but for investors, all that activity just increases expenses.

Think of it this way: Every time an investor reallocates investments within his/her equity or bond portfolio, what they really do is shift a small portion of their assets to a brokerage firm (Wall Street). Why else would they tell us to do that at least once a year? Sure, there is sound reasoning for reallocation based on financial theory supported by empirical data, but the result is still the same. Wall Street wins. The house always wins, especially when we listen to house advice and follow house guidance.

Thus, instead of trying to be in the right sector at the right time, I try to be in the right stock for the long haul, knowing that there will be speed bumps and setbacks along the way but also knowing that the laws of time and compounding will eventually work out in my favor if I have selected well. That is one of the key underpinnings of investing, as far as I am concerned. Selectivity, compounding, rising dividends, and value. Combine those four concepts, and you end up in a good place somewhere down the road.

Selectivity

What do I mean by selectivity? In my process, I start by developing a list of companies that I would like to own if the prices of the respective stocks ever reach extreme value levels.

I rate companies within industries to identify those that qualify for further consideration. Basically, what I look for are companies that consistently stand head and shoulders above the competition. Companies on my list pay dividends with a yield equal to or higher than average for the industry while maintaining a payout ratio at or below the industry average. One should not look at one of those factors without the other. I also want my list of companies to have debt-to-equity ratios at or below the industry average, consistently rising dividends and higher-than-industry-average growth in both revenue and earnings. To land on my list, a company must maintain a credit rating of investment grade or have little or no debt, and it must have positive free cash flow. A company that does not generate free cash flow needs either to sell more stock (diluting investors: not good) or is too dependent upon debt to maintain operations. Free cash flow generation, combined with below-average debt (for the industry), provides a company with greater flexibility to invest in expanding operations or to consider acquisitions to provide added future growth. The only exception to the rules on debt and free cash flow is for regulated industries, where those companies can price services or products such that the company will generate a consistent return on invested capital.

Once I have the list from all industries that I at least think I understand, I consider qualitative aspects of management and business models. I also consider the long-term sustainability of the industry and try to shy away from those industries that are under attack (or likely to be so) from disruptive technologies or changes in cultural/societal perceptions. Think coal, movie theaters (streaming is causing problems), cable television, or processed foods. Public perceptions change over time. Identifying the shifts can help avoid some pain.

On the positive side, I look for companies that have developed a moat to defend their position against competition. Some moats are stronger than others. Patents and proprietary technologies are great for as long as they last. Consistently staying ahead of competition through innovation is also great for as long as it lasts (think Intel and Cisco Systems in the 1990s). Corporate culture can be a huge advantage or a huge barrier. A brand that is recognized the world over and is associated with positive images and values that consumers admire can be a powerful way to differentiate and provide a competitive advantage. When a brand gets tarnished, it is hard to rise back to a dominant position. But companies that have exhibited the ability to do so in the past are likely to be able to do so again in the future, and when things look bleak for such companies, there is often excellent value.

International Business Machines (NYSE: IBM) is a fitting example. Some readers will not remember how badly IBM managed the shift from mainframe computers to minicomputers to desktop computers. The company's products had been considered top-of-the-line for decades, but competition caught up and passed it by in many areas. The culture that had made the company successful in the past was holding it back from entering the future at full speed. It fell behind the curve, and the brand was tarnished relative to its previous position. Then, management was caught using aggressive accounting practices to book revenue on systems that had been built and shipped to distribution warehouses as part of sales, having not yet found buyers for the product. This practice finally caught up to it, and the company had to adjust its financial reports and accounting practices. However, IBM finally reorganized itself and focused on services and software instead of hardware. It took time, but the transformation was a tremendous success. The brand was back. Today, the company is going through some more problems, and the question of whether it will be able to transform again is still unanswered. The problems could get worse before they get better from here. So, IBM, which made my list in the past, is now back on probation until it proves that it can do the phoenix-rising thing again.

I will offer more examples in the book and hope that the details will be instructive. The bottom line is that, because of my overall investing strategy, I rarely pay much attention to how much I have in any one sector or industry. In truth, I just wait for what I consider to be bargain entry points and buy what I believe will provide reliable income growth over the long term.

Interlude 2: The Janitor

Ronald Read, of Brattleboro, Vermont, died at the age of 92 in June of 2014, leaving an estate valued at $8 million is not bad for a janitor.

Mr. Read lived a very modest life and saved as much as he could. He also invested and accumulated what, to most of us, would be a fortune. He lived his life in Vermont, with his only extended period away being his service in World War II, where he saw action in both North Africa and the Pacific.

After the war, he returned to Brattleboro and worked for his brother at a gas station for 25 years before retiring. He apparently did not enjoy retirement because he chose instead to work as a janitor at a J.C. Penny's store until 1997.

He was a patient investor. By that I mean that he did not trade in and out of stocks. His estate included a stack of stock certificates five inches thick that he had kept in a safe deposit box. By holding the certificates, as was more customary in his day, he required a multi-step process to sell any of his stock. He would have to go down to the bank and access his safe deposit box to retrieve the certificate and then travel to the brokerage office to turn in the certificate to be sold. Compare that to a couple of clicks on a computer or swipes on a smartphone today. Convenience has turned investing into trading these days. As referenced elsewhere in this book, trading is not a good strategy for most people. Too often, it leads to failure and the loss of an entire nest egg that took many years to accumulate.

Mr. Read had two things in his favor: patience and time. He rarely, if ever, sold stock that he held. He also lived to be 92 years old. If you recall the earlier tables, you will realize how much the compounding effect impacted his results in his later years. He had held many of his stocks for several decades. It is amazing just how much accumulation goes on after the first 20 years of investing and even more so after 30 years.

Another of Ronald's keys to success was that he bought dividend-paying stocks: railroads, utilities, banks, healthcare, telecom, and consumer products companies. He then reinvested the dividends into more shares of those same stocks. He was not an active trader, but he was an active buyer, especially later in life. All those dividend checks gave him the ability to make regular purchases. But it was the early purchases, the foundation that he built early in life, which made it all possible.

In the end, his portfolio included the stocks of 95 companies, mostly blue chips. Among those were household names like Smucker's (SJM), J.P. Morgan-Chase (JPM), Procter & Gamble (PG), Johnson & Johnson (JNJ), CVS Health (CVS), and Dow Chemical (DOW). He also owned Lehman Brothers (which went bankrupt), but his diversified portfolio spread and limited the risk of loss, so the impact of his failed holdings was offset by the successes.

During his life, Mr. Read had to pay taxes on his dividends, but since there was no record of his ever selling a stock, he paid no taxes on his gains. Mr. Read was a widower and bequeathed his millions to the local hospital and library. The IRS got almost nothing relative to the size of his estate. A janitor who was wise beyond his externally apparent means.

Part III:
Creating a Plan to Achieve Financial Security

Chapter 14:
Understanding Your Investing Time Horizon

Time Horizons

The reason this is important is simply because you do not want to outlive your retirement savings. I want to begin this chapter with a few questions that need to be answered before each investor can realistically understand what to plan for prior to developing a plan.

1. What is my expected holding period?

2. How do I plan for emergency issues and build that into my plan?

3. Which asset presents the best value when I have the cash to invest?

4. What are my long-term goals, and how will each asset help me achieve those goals?

Before one decides what to buy, one must understand what they will need at the end of their investing horizon to carry them through to the end (however you want to define that; and, before you laugh, it is different for everyone). Some people want to set up a charitable foundation that will give money for a cause eternally. Some just want to retire and enjoy life, travel, and relax. Others may want to get their kids off to a good start or help ensure that they have something for later in life, too. Still, others may want to help grandchildren with college expenses. How about a new sailboat or that recreational vehicle?

Yet others want to do it all and cannot be realistic about the decisions that need to be made to get there. Some have it all covered, some have a good start, and some are dreadfully behind where they need to be. It may seem too late for a few, but with good planning, reasonable goals, and consistent execution, most folks can at least retire comfortably (even if it means working a few years longer than originally planned). However, the place to start is by determining one's investing horizons. I will start off by explaining mine.

I am 75 years of age now, but I still have a long-term view regarding my investments. My wife and I are getting to the point where we will begin to use some of the income from our retirement accounts within the next few years, even though I have been "officially" retired since 2002. I expect to live another 10 years or more; my wife will probably outlive me, and we both would like to leave something for our two children to make it a little easier for them later in life. So, with that in mind, I need to invest with the idea that my savings need to last well into the retirement years of my children, ages 29 and 33. That gives me three time horizons to consider:

1. First, I need to have adequate funds set aside to meet our living expenses and my final expenses (sorry, but death does not always come cheap). My life insurance should help supplement the final expenses. The rest will need to come from savings. My wife cared for her mother in our home for several years. She had me around to help with the lifting, or it could have caused her health issues. Hospice was also helpful. Choosing that route conserved a good deal of her mother's savings. My mother wanted to remain in Corpus Christi, Texas (half a continent away), so she spent her remaining three years in a retirement center with multiple levels of care available. Her living costs escalated from about $4,000 per month to just over $6,000 per month near the end (and that was nearly two decades ago, so it would be much more now). Then, of course, there were the final medical costs and funeral arrangements. Both of our mothers passed quickly (within days) of becoming ill. So, the costs were relatively minimal. Still, the additional cost over the status quo can be substantial. It varies greatly depending on the choices we make, how long we live after losing the ability to care for ourselves, and medical conditions. This is not the sort of thing that is easily quantified or pleasant to think about, but we all need to talk it through with a spouse or likely caregiver and make the hard choices ahead of time. Then, we need to remember to provide for the financial part; otherwise, it could create an unnecessary burden on loved ones.

2. Next, I need to make sure that the funds, after being partially depleted by my end of life, will be adequate to provide for my wife's living expenses and her final expenses. Fortunately, she will still be covered by my health insurance, and my remaining pension will cover that cost for the rest of her life. The usual plan is to have a life insurance policy to cover her final expenses. If she outlives the term of the coverage and extending the policy is too expensive, the expenses will need to come out of her estate.

3. How much do we want to leave to the kids, and how much do we want to give away? Sorry, but those are more personal questions and will be different for each individual reader. Just be aware that I need to plan to provide the funds to make our wishes possible over the remainder of my lifetime. My wife may be lost on the investing front and will err on the side of caution. That is not a bad thing. I will move systematically toward that end over the next 10 years to make the transition easier for her.

I think I have outlined the goals my wife and I have set for ourselves in the preceding discussion about horizons. But I will drill a little deeper to make it easier to apply for those who desire to do so.

First off, we have a comfortable existence, living on about $6,500 per month. Our house still has a mortgage, and with a 2.75% interest rate, we will probably keep it, assuming I live as long as I expect. If we choose to move to a smaller home, we will rent our current home for income. The basement is finished and has a bedroom, bathroom, and large living room area. It could be rented for about $900 per month. The upstairs will be rented for $2,500. Those amounts should rise at or above the rate of inflation.

That will raise our income further above our expenses, so we will not need to dip into retirement savings.

When my wife finds herself living alone, she will probably move into a retirement center or remain in the smaller house, assuming we move together while I am still around. Her expenses will either rise or fall significantly, depending on her choice. If she opts to move into a retirement center, her expenses could be in the $6,000 per month range or higher. She can keep her expenses lower by downsizing if she prefers to conserve what principal savings are left. I cannot speculate as to which route she will take since, after being together for nearly 40 years, I have found foretelling my wife's decisions is not a profitable venture. But I still need to plan for her future needs.

There are a lot of contingencies in this that I will not go into because it just gets too morbid and boring to write about or read. I include this only because it is part of the deal. If you are not including such things in your plans, you are either way ahead of me (financially) or living on hope.

Plan for the Expected and the Unexpected

In case you have not noticed yet, I am working backward from what will be needed in the end toward what we will need in between and, finally, what we need now. Whatever age you are, you need to have an emergency cash cushion. I will explain the mechanics of how I use this tool in a later chapter, but suffice it to say that there will be things requiring cash throughout life, sometimes planned and other times (more often than you may think) entirely unexpected. As the name "emergency" implies, this one is for those unforeseen situations that are not planned. The rule of thumb is to keep at least three to six months of living expenses to fall back on; we prefer more in the range of nine to twelve months. I know I am being overly conservative here, but I like having flexibility, as I will explain later.

In addition to the unexpected outlays that come out of nowhere, we also need to plan to have funds available for those planned instances, such as a new car (down payment and monthly payments), new furniture or appliances, a down payment on that first home (if you are still renting or just starting out) and moving expenses. The list could be longer for some and shorter for others, depending on where you are in life and what your desires are. But the fact of the matter is that we need to plan for these things and have the cash available when we need it.

Relying too much on credit will just dig a financial hole where you do not want to find yourself. Always pay off your credit card bills in full every month. If you have high-interest debt, forget about saving until it is paid off completely. Then, start saving for planned purchases by setting aside money each month while also creating an emergency cash cushion. After that is all in place, then you can start investing. If you are ever going to live comfortably in retirement, you first need to learn how to live within your means today and every day. Prioritize and take care of the basics first.

Chapter Summary Review

Get a sense of how much you will need to cover end-of-life expenses, including higher costs for assisted care and medical expenses. Understand that you will need a lump-sum amount available to cover the final costs, but you also need to have regular income to afford the care you want and deserve. I will explain how to invest so that you can cover both later in the book.

Make sure you are prepared for emergencies that arise unexpectedly by building a cash cushion equal to at least three to six months of your current living expenses.

Set aside cash for future planned purchases and be honest with yourself about how much you will need and when you will need it. This can be invested conservatively in short-term instruments that are not likely to lose principal value to help build and provide income.

Before you start investing, make certain that you are living within your means and have no outstanding high-interest debt. Get your house in order before you start building a portfolio. Eliminating the high-interest payments will reduce your overall expenses in the long term and allow you to keep more of what you earn.

Chapter 15:
Investing for Income Works!

Income Sources Matter

This brings me to a particularly critical point that I mentioned earlier about investing for future income rather than just appreciation. I have found that if I buy a quality asset that meets my income requirements and fulfills my future expectations, appreciation occurs as a result. I used to focus solely on appreciation potential. That turned out to be a haphazard proposition. Investing for future income has worked much better. Most asset values are based, to some degree or another, on the level of income that is provided, especially relative to other similar assets. I will get into the relative valuation of assets later.

For me, it all comes down to how much income I will need to support my future goals. This is especially true for investors just starting out early in life. If I set a dollar amount that I think I will need, say, $1 million, how do I know that it will provide the income I need in the future when I want to endure less risk in my investment portfolio? If you plan to move to more bonds or other forms of fixed income during retirement, which is the "normal" route investors are told to take, how much will I be earning if at age 65 I have accumulated $1 million but 30-year Treasuries are only yielding about 1.6 percent? I can only count on $16,000 of annual income if I convert it all to a Treasury portfolio. If you had told most people 30 years ago that the yield on 30-year U.S. Treasury bonds would be under 1.6 percent someday, they would have called you crazy. But that is where we were in the recent past and could be again in the future! So, $1 million may not be enough!

Of course, you can add more risk of loss to your portfolio by adding corporate bonds, which is not usually a bad move if you stick to companies with investment-grade credit ratings, but your income may still not meet your needs. The yields are better, though. And dropping down into junk-rated bonds is too risky because bonds trade up and down in price in relation to the economic cycle, for my taste, as the risk of loss rises considerably should the economy enter a recession. Earning five or six percent per year will no longer seem so good when the principal value of your bonds falls by 20 percent or more or a few of your bond holdings default or the parent company files for bankruptcy.

At this point, the yield on long-term bonds does not appeal to me. Plain and simple. If inflation comes back, interest rates will rise, and the yield on bonds may become more enticing again. I do not expect to see double-digit yields on Treasuries like we experienced in the late 1970s and into the 1980s. But I do expect to see inflation tick higher over the next decade, averaging closer to 3%, so interest on high-quality, long-term bonds should rise closer to 5% to 7% at some point. Then, I will reconsider investing in bonds again.

You may wonder why I expect inflation to average near 3% when the Fed target is 2%. The answer is not simple, but to summarize: 1) the long-term average of inflation in the U.S. has been closer to 3% than 2%, and 2) my study of demographics in the U.S. tells me that we are entering a period of higher inflation due to generational shifts to consumption patterns that will play out over the next several decades.

Investors should keep in mind that investing in bonds for income requires funds that will not be needed until maturity unless yields are falling. Why? As interest rates rise, the principal (price) of bonds falls, and the longer the maturity, the more the price will move. It was a fun ride holding bonds when interest rates fell from over 5% in 2007 to lows below 2% since that led to significant capital gains. But when the trend changes and starts heading in the opposite direction, it can be a miserable experience. The result could be disastrous for anyone who may need access to cash from their bond holdings before maturity. The losses could be hefty. So, I would not buy bonds in a market with money that may be needed for other purposes prior to the bond maturity until I am sure that interest rates are more apt to fall than rise.

Investing for Income

For my purposes, it has become a matter of investing to add another layer of rising future income. Still, one must be very selective and avoid overpaying for equity securities. There can be fewer bargains in an aging bull market. Sometimes, it makes more sense to sit on cash, earning interest below the rate of inflation, than risking a significant loss to principal. This is one of the most difficult things an investor can do. But it has paid off handsomely in the past, and I would expect it to do so repeatedly as the market trend changes from bull to bear over time. The thing to keep in mind is that the extremely long-term trend of stocks is up. So, patience pays off over time.

I will address how I select stocks in a later chapter but try to visualize buying a stock that pays a dividend and raises that dividend by 6% or more year after year. Then, imagine buying another stock with the same potential. Then, adding another and another. Now imagine having bought stocks over a lifetime, building up layer upon layer of dividend income that rises every year. The eventual annual income can be nearly as much as the initial cost of the stock after a few decades. Think about that for a minute: you could be earning more each year than you originally invested in total, with the expectation of your income rising each year for as long as you live. Let that soak in for a moment.

That is the combination of the power of investing for income and the power of compound interest! As Warren Buffett once called it: "The eighth wonder of the world!"

The time is nearing again when bonds will be my preferred investment for income, but it could be several years before yields reach my minimum requirement. That reminds me of the experience I mentioned earlier about helping friends save for future college expenses. At that time, bonds were the best solution to their investing needs. To maximize return and future income, investors need to be flexible in terms of which asset type they use depending upon the economic environment at any given time.

When bond yields are high (relative to stock yields) and more likely to fall than rise over the next five to ten years, then bonds are a worthwhile investment. As yields fall, bond prices rise (and vice versa), and the value of a bond held during a period of falling interest rates increases. But when interest rates are low and more likely to rise in the future, expect the value of bonds to drop, so stay away. I realize that I have mentioned this several times already, but it is important enough of a concept that you really need to understand the principle. Repetition of a foreign concept helps build memory.

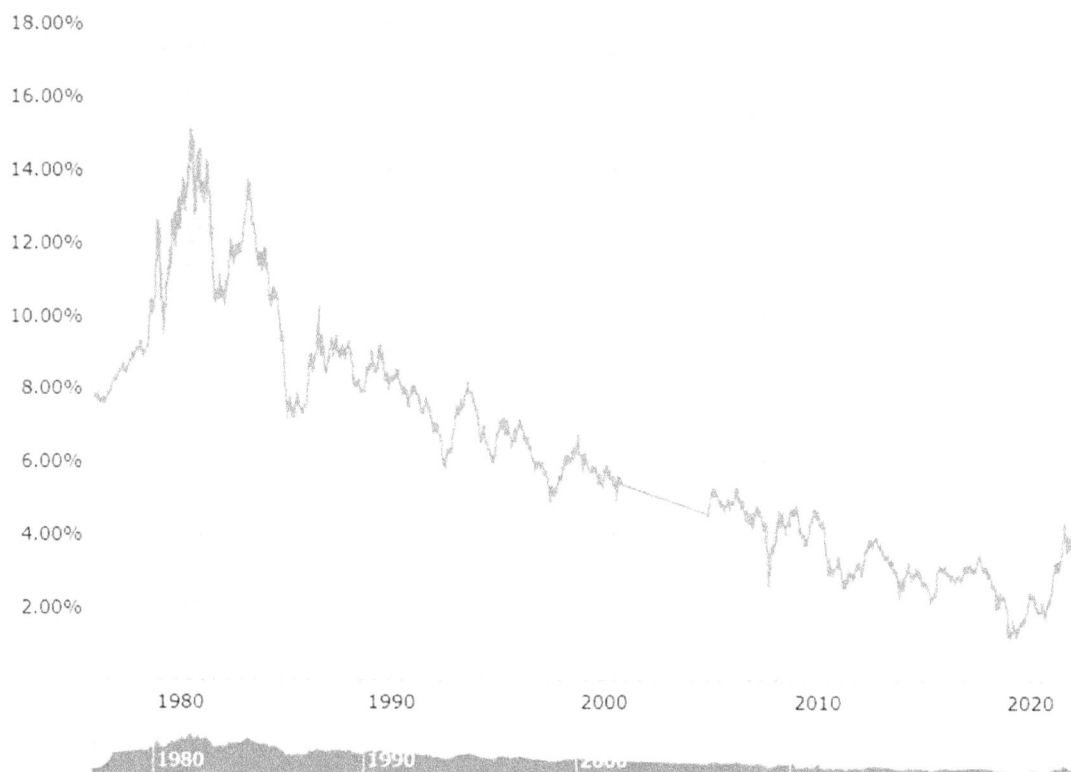

Source: Macro Trends[7]

Bonds will once again be a great investment for everyone. As recently as a couple of years ago, those securities were primarily used by those needing immediate income without the risk inherent in stocks and who plan to hold the bonds to maturity. The other use is to diversify a portfolio, but when rates were at a historically low level and trending higher, it seemed less able to provide the stability that would be afforded with higher, or more normal, interest rates. Now that the trend toward normalization has begun, bonds should be more appetizing to a broader group of investors in the not-too-distant future.

However, the point of this story is about understanding the investment vehicle being used, the likely outcome, having a plan, and sticking to it to reap the benefits. The key to investing for income is patience and selectivity. Let us look at another true story to drive this concept home.

---

[7] https://www.macrotrends.net/2521/30-year-treasury-bond-rate-yield-chart

Chapter 16:
The Man Who Built a
Fortune Systematically in Real Estate

Back in the 1970s, while I was still in college, I had a co-worker who confided in me about his plan to reach financial freedom. He was in his early 40s at the time and well on his way to reaching his goal of retiring at 55.

He started out buying a house to live in near the university campus and his work. When he found out how much the house next door was rented for, he decided to buy another house and move out so he could rent his. The rent was much more than his monthly mortgage payment, so he spotted the opportunity right away. But his long-term plan had still not emerged.

He was a postal worker; it was then the early 1970s, and he was making enough money to save a down payment for another house every three years. Houses were far cheaper than they are today, but mortgage rates were higher (usually above 8%). I'm not sure how much he bought each house for or exactly how much he was making when he started out, but I do know that while I was in college and working for the postal service, I was making about $12,000 or more (with overtime) per year in 1974.

To put things into perspective, I could have bought a 3-bedroom, one-bath home for under $20,000. The average new car price was between $3,000 and $4,000, while a new Volkswagen Beetle was priced at $1,999. Saving for a down payment on a house was easier back then, even though wages were also lower. The cost of living was much lower, as well.

It soon dawned on him that if he just kept buying another rental property whenever he had enough for the down payment, he could end up with 20-30 rental properties by the time he retired, and some of them would be fully paid off.

Every few years, the time it took to accumulate another down payment grew shorter because each house he had purchased provided free cash flow that he could save toward the next downpayment. The more houses he owned, the more money he could save because he never bought a house for a price and mortgage rate that would not provide positive cash flow. That was the key: free cash flow.

By the time I met him, he already owned nine houses and was able to buy another one each year (if he could find one that would cash flow). For a rental property to cash flow, you need the monthly rent to exceed the mortgage payment by more than enough to cover maintenance, repairs, replacements, and temporary vacancies. He figured that out early on and rarely made a mistake.

He was in a college town where there was always a ready market for renters. Any mistakes he made were in choosing his tenants, but he got better at that over time, too. He always made sure that the parents were parties to the rental agreements in case damage occurred, and the contracts were always for a full year. All property owners in the area did the same thing, so the students (and their respective parents) had little choice but to agree.

Back then, he could get by with $100 per month per unit for maintenance, repairs, and replacements. That number went up over time. So, if he knew he could rent a house for at least $150 a month more than the mortgage payment, he felt sure he would have enough cash flow to help him save for the next down payment.

So far, it sounds much easier than it really was, but his plan had a method. As the years progressed, he was able to raise rents a little higher, making the early purchases able to generate even more free cash flow. By the time we met, his first rental property was already generating several hundred dollars per month that he could save or reinvest. By the time he reached retirement age of 55, he expected to have two or three houses completely paid off, collecting about 90 percent of the rent to use for his own living costs. The rent would have about doubled by that time. He would also have a pension from the government after more than 30 years of service (almost 60% of his pay at the time of retirement), so the money from rentals would more than offset the loss of income from not working.

To make it even more interesting, after being retired for about ten years, he would have another house paid off each year (no more mortgage), increasing his monthly income by several hundred dollars per month each year for many years.

Here are some things to remember if you invest in real estate.

First, if you are going to err on the maintenance, repairs, and replacements, do so on the high side. If you plan to hold onto a rental property long-term, you will need to replace the HVAC system (heating, ventilation, and air conditioning), the roof, floor covering, light fixtures, and appliances (several times for appliances). You will need to repair holes in the walls and paint regularly. The lawn will need to be mowed, and if you get snow, you will need to remove snow from walkways and parking. Whenever renters move out, it is always a clever idea to change the keying of all outside locks. You should also keep the water and sewer in your name and pay those costs because you do not want those to be shut off if a renter falls behind. That leads to legal battles you do not need.

Make sure you keep a fund set aside for the unexpected because something will happen when you least expect it. You should identify reliable and reasonably priced handyman services, electricians, and plumbers. Do not scrimp on maintaining the HVAC system. It will cost less overall if properly maintained because it will be more efficient and last longer. Whenever you make an offer, include a home inspection contingency. To find a good inspector (and other reliable workers), ask multiple realtors in the area with rental management experience for recommendations. Walk through the house and grounds with the inspector to make sure s/he is thorough. You will be surprised at how much you might learn.

If you find good, non-student renters and want to keep them longer term, do not raise rents as much as other landlords. It is easier to keep a good renter than to find another one. And vacancies are a cost also. Do not forget to include a reasonable vacancy rate for your area in your planned budget. How much will depend on whether you charge the maximum rent for the area or are most reasonably priced. If you charge $50 a month less than comparable rentals in the area, you will receive less monthly rent, but you may receive more rent per year by avoiding tenant turnover. If you need to charge a higher rent to make your budget work, you probably paid too much for the property.

When interest rates are high, property prices usually come down. The monthly mortgage payment may be higher than you would like in the beginning, but remember that you should be able to refinance at a lower rate later, making the property cash flow much better over time. Bargains can be had in buyer markets (when real estate sales are slower and buyers have more negotiating power).

When interest rates are low (as they were in 2021), you can pay more for the house, and it can still generate free cash flow. I'll give you an example. In the summer of 2021, I bought a house for my family to live in, and we started with a mortgage payment of about $1,550 a month. Before we bought the house, it was rented by a family for $2,200 a month. It is amazing how much difference a mortgage interest rate of 2.75% can make! My first rental property had an interest rate of around 8.5%. The new home has four bedrooms and 3 ½ baths. The house next door is much smaller and has two bedrooms and two baths, but it now rents for $3,000 per month. We bought it at an opportune time and will probably hold onto the house long term (as a rental), even if we move again.

One last story about the best rental property deal I ever made. I mentioned this in an earlier chapter but feel it merits repeating with a little more detail. While we were living in Alamosa, Colorado, I found a 4-plex listed for $105,000. It had four two-bedroom units and four single-car garage spaces. One unit was vacant. I used my VA loan guarantee since I had served in the Army and got the property with no down payment. We closed on about the 3rd of the month, so rent had been paid. I received a check at closing because the prorated rents were more than my closing costs. My wife and I moved in and found that the rent from the three rented units covered the mortgage payment. We just had to pay for the water, sewer, electricity, and maintenance. It was not quite completely rent-free, but close.

That was in 1986, and the units were rented for $325 per month. Today, the property has more than tripled in value, and rents have increased at a similar rate. When we moved out, the rent from the 4th unit was more than enough to cover maintenance, repairs, and replacements, and the tax breaks back then were also more generous than today. So, it produced free cash flow from the beginning and is completely paid off today. The monthly free cash flow is over $3,000 after maintenance, repairs, and replacement, which is squirreled away in a separate account from the rent.

Interlude 3

The Teacher

Kathleen McGowan, a first-grade schoolteacher for 35 years, retired in 1984. She never married and lived well within her means. She invested in dividend-paying stocks and reinvested much, if not all, of the dividend proceeds consistently over her life.

Kathleen's twin brother, Robert, moved into the family home with his sister after retiring from a career in insurance and helped her invest her savings. Between the two of them, they had accumulated more than $10 million by the time they passed away. Kathleen's estate was $6 million, most of which was donated to her 15 favorite causes.

No one knew that Kathleen was a millionaire while she was alive because of her frugal lifestyle. She lived to be 84 years old, providing another example of how compounding over time works. She could have enjoyed the fruits of her labor and investing during her retirement, but she preferred to live a simple life.

According to the attorney who handled her estate, Kathleen never looked at her portfolio because she had no need for it for personal use. She just let it accumulate and reinvested the cash that flowed from it year after year.

Those 15 charities reaped the benefits of her investing acumen and patience. Kathleen, a career elementary school teacher, left behind a legacy that touched the lives of many, both during her working years and for many years after.

Part IV:
Understanding Wall Street

Chapter 17:
The Wall Street Agenda

Whose Side Are They On?

As I have stated before in this book, Wall Street is not always on your side. In fact, the agenda of most Wall Street executives is to make money, not for you, but for themselves! There are some who are truly trying their best to make your money grow, though. The problem is they are not particularly good at doing so. Historically, less than 20% of fund managers beat the returns of the S&P 500 Index in any given year. Even fewer can outperform the index consistently. However, they do much better than most individual investors.

The Two Types of Wall Street Analysts

There are two types of analysts on Wall Street: The Buy Side analysts and the Sell Side analysts.

Buyside analysts are those who represent fund management and are usually more reliable and honest. The reason for this distinction is that the fund managers make money based upon performance of the funds they manage (your money) and need to keep you invested in those funds to grow their respective business incomes. They charge a management fee based on the amount of AUM (assets under management). If investors withdraw money from the fund(s) managed the manager (and his firm) cannot receive fees on those funds. So, they have a vested interest in buying and recommending stocks they truly believe will outperform the overall market over time. They are not always right in the short term, but they have a decent track record over longer periods.

Sell-side analysts represent the brokerage firms that make money by selling stocks and managing assets for wealthy clients. These analysts have a different agenda from the buy-side analysts. The sell-side firms are focused on helping their corporate clients sell stocks to the public and make money for their wealthy clients. They are not as concerned about what happens to small investors like you and me. These are the analysts who rarely change a stock's rating from buy to sell until after the stock has already fallen, and this is the primary reason that many small investors sell at the worst possible time.

Trading Desks

The major banks usually have trading desks or rooms full of people who trade on behalf of the bank to make a small profit on large transactions many times per day. The banks also employ algorithms that will automatically initiate trades when certain technical indicators flash buy or sell. The volumes of shares traded by these algorithms can be huge. Hedge funds, another form of Wal Street players, also employ algorithms for trading. These day-trading groups can account for more than 60%, on average, of all trade volume on any given day. They claim to create stability, but I think they create more intraday volatility.

Manipulation

We all know it happens, but we cannot prove it because those who control all the evidence are the perpetrators. They can initiate a trade for millions of shares in a fraction of a second and then cancel the trade before it is completed, creating a momentary fluctuation in imaginary demand for a particular stock and causing other investors to act. This is one form of market manipulation that happens.

Another well-known type of manipulation is when analysts attempt to move the stock of a company with comments in the media, either positive or negative, to either find a better buy price or a better sell price for their wealthy clients. They may upgrade a stock to convince more investors to buy while selling shares for their clients before later downgrading the stock. However, the sell-side analysts rarely downgrade a stock until after it has fallen significantly, thereby making the timing of the information useless to the public.

Financial Advisors

Very few financial advisors working for large brokerage firms have much in-depth training, especially in their early years within the industry, about finance and investing. Most rely on the analysts at the home office to provide investment ideas and portfolio recommendations for their clients. Most start out as salespeople who have studied the laws that govern securities markets and financial advisors. It is not difficult, and there are no educational requirements.

Conclusion

Wall Street is focused on making money for itself, not the small, individual investors. If you have a proven method and stick to it, you are better off managing your own money. But that takes time. Sometimes, it is just more efficient and responsible to hire someone you can trust to manage your money. Finding someone you can trust can take some time, but it is time well spent. Do not hurry into a relationship with a financial advisor. Vet them carefully or ask friends who use them about how well they have done for them. A CFA (Chartered Financial Analyst) means that they have at least been through a rigorous testing process that lasts three or more years and requires a lot of study.

However, even a CFA does not guarantee success. They still need to be vetted, and you should make certain that your financial advisor agrees with your approach to investing. If you want to own dividend-paying stocks that increase the dividend every year, but your advisor is buying stocks that do not pay dividends for your account, you should revisit your selection or have a meeting with your advisor to ensure that you both have the same long-term investment objectives.

Chapter 18:
The Reality of Different Investing Styles

Defining Styles of Investing

There are many investing styles to choose from. Some may seem to overlap with other styles.

Combining more than one style for separate portions of a portfolio is fine, but it is best to stick with what works best for you and makes you feel most comfortable. Do not mix and match within segmented portions of a portfolio.

I will explain some of the most popular styles and then introduce my personal investing style to you. Some of the most common high-level investing styles are:

Active or Passive

These are two styles of investing that usually pertain to professional money managers. Active managers typically have a staff of financial researchers or analysts who carefully select the holdings of the fund being managed. Actively managed funds charge higher fees for their services. Even then, only about 20 percent of all actively managed funds consistently outperformed the S&P 500 Index.

This brings us to passive investment management. Passively managed funds try to mimic an index or sector performance, such as the S&P 500 Index or one of the 11 sectors of the stock market. With passive management, you get all the gyrations of the market, but you do not miss major moves by holding cash or being invested in the wrong stocks.

As an individual investor, you can choose to manage your own portfolio using either of the styles above. Active management requires a lot of time, or you pay someone to do the analysis for you. If your portfolio is on the small side (under $100,000), paying for high-quality analysis may be too expensive, so allowing a professional to manage your funds could cost you less.

However, active management will usually cost 1% (or more) of your portfolio each year, so when you have amassed a sizeable sum in your portfolio, it starts to get expensive. Of course, if you manage it yourself and make major mistakes, it could cost you even more.

A solid, rules-based approach to managing your own portfolio can help you avoid those costly mistakes. However, even just keeping up with the overall average gains of the S&P 500 will work well for investors over the long term.

Growth Investing

Investing for growth can be achieved in many ways, but the growth investing style means investing in fast-growing companies. To find companies that are expected to grow faster than the overall market, investors use a set of metrics (the set varies from one money manager to another), such as high earnings growth, high revenue growth, high return on equity, or high profit margins, to name a few.

Not all metrics work to identify companies with the best growth prospects. I like to use FCF (free cash flow) to find companies with future growth prospects. If a company does not generate FCF, it means the company will either need to issue more shares (diluting existing shareholders) or raise capital by issuing debt. Either way, it is not sustainable over an extended period. I will include more about FCF investing in a future chapter.

Value Investing

Value investors look for companies that have a strong financial foundation at a bargain price. Too often, investors make the mistake of selecting companies with low P/E (price to earnings) ratios or high dividends as being bargains, only to find out that there are reasons those companies' stocks are "cheap." Inferior performance or disruptive forces upending a company's business model can make a formerly great company look cheap. Value investing requires research and analysis, as well, to be successful.

Small Cap Investing

This is exactly what it sounds like: investing in companies with total market capitalization (the total number of shares outstanding multiplied by the share price) between $300 million and $2 billion. The idea behind small-cap investing is that the mega-companies are already so big that they cannot grow as fast as a small company. But that perception is often very wrong. Large-cap companies tend to acquire smaller competitors with higher growth potential. So, if a small company in which you own shares is acquired by a large company, you could receive a windfall because the acquisition price is usually at a premium to the current market price of the company being acquired. However, this also requires small companies to be successful and sustainable. A lot of small companies go out of business long before meeting the expectations of early investors. In other words, small-cap investing is much riskier than many other styles.

Large Cap Investing

Again, there is no secret meaning: this is just investing in companies with a market capitalization of more than $10 billion. Large companies often (not always) generate FCF, reliable profit margins, and have competitive advantages over smaller companies in the same or related industries. Advantages may include lower costs, broader distribution channels, brand loyalty, and patented products or processes (to name a few). The idea behind large-cap investing is that revenue and profit forecasting is more reliable and sustainable. This is often true, but not always. Again, it is important that even large companies are generating FCF on a sustainable basis to support funding needed for future growth.

There are many other styles of investing, but those are the main ones. Companies of all sizes may become dependent on debt to finance their ongoing operations. When debt is cheap (low-interest rate environment), it is easier to stay in business, even for companies that would otherwise not be able to sustain themselves without regular borrowing. Always make sure that companies can sustain operations and grow without adding debt (except regulated companies) or that the company generates enough FCF to service the existing debt.

My personal style is to look for companies that are leaders in their respective industries and have sustainable competitive advantages that pay dividends that rise consistently every year for at least the last ten years (I really prefer 25 years of rising dividends, but some excellent companies do not have that many years of dividend paying history). I also look for consistently superior performance relative to their peers in areas such as revenue growth, profit margin, FCF generation, dividend yield, history of dividend increases, total debt to total assets, and debt credit rating. If a company is average or better than average in all those criteria over at least five years compared to its industry peers, it fits my definition of quality.

Free Cash Flow (FCF)

The other piece of my investing style is finding quality at bargain prices. This requires a valuation assessment, but it can be a remarkably simple one. Before I buy the stock of a company, I look at two valuations. You can use only one if you are comfortable with the methodology. Many investors rely on the PE (Price to Earnings) ratio, but this does not tell us if the company is really of any value. It merely tells us if it is cheap relative to current earnings (which may be inflated by gains on asset sales or changes in accounting). It can be a place to start, but it is not the best method of valuation.

I use FCF analysis as my primary method of identifying bargains. I define free cash flow using a method similar to what Berkshire Hathaway's Warren Buffett uses when analyzing companies:

Net Income + Depreciation + Amortization – Capital Expenditures = Free Cash Flow

Then, I divide the market price of the stock by FCF per share and produce a ratio. Anything below 15 is a bargain, and anything above 30 is overpriced.

But there is a catch. I require the company to be consistent in generating strong FCF and fitting my definition of quality for at least five consecutive years. Without consistency, there is a lesser probability of sustainable future growth. I will explain more about FCF analysis in a later chapter.

Dividend Discount Model

Finally, I plug the company numbers into my variation on the dividend discount model (DDM), using a minimum required rate of return (which I vary from one industry to another because all industries are not created equal and cannot provide the same returns over time) as the discount rate. It may seem a little unorthodox, but it has worked well for me. The Excel equation I use is:

=(D/(M-X))

D = Current dividend

M = discount rate (or I use a minimum required return on investment)

X = expected future average annual increase in dividend

As an example, if we look at Air Products and Chemicals (APD), we see that the dividend per share is $7.00 (June 2023), the expected future average annual increase in dividend is 7.8% (I get this from SeekingAlpha.com). Plugging a required minimum rate of return of 10%, we get a formula of:

($7.00 / (10% - 7.8%)) = $318.18

The share price was about $281 (on June 2, 2023), so from a DDM perspective, the share price is reasonable or, a little low, but not a real bargain.

If you look at the PE ratio of 28.9, it is high relative to its industry peers (12.8) and above the long-term average for the company. It is almost equal to the five-year average, but most of that period included extremely low interest rates, which tend to boost valuations. So, if interest rates remain elevated for more than a year, we can expect valuations, such as PE ratios, to decrease to reflect the new higher cost of capital. That will require prices to fall to normalize valuations.

As far as the FCF analysis is concerned, the Price to FCF ratio is 28 (at the time of this writing). Therefore, APD is no real bargain since it is close to being overvalued (a ratio of 30 or above). To be a bargain, the ratio would need to be below 15. APD stock was rated as a hold.

Chapter 19:
Why I Prefer Individual Stocks and ETFs Over Mutual Funds

Put your money to work...

Not in someone else's pocket! When you invest in a stock mutual fund, there is usually a front-end load (fee to be shared by brokerage and your advisor) that is often as high as 5.75%. So, when you invest in a mutual fund with a "load," you are not investing all your money. You are investing less than 95% of it, and you start out in the hole!

You will be told that you are benefiting from "professional" management by the experienced fund manager(s). True. However, you should also remember that less than 20% of fund managers beat the S&P 500 Index in any given year, and even fewer than that can beat the index consistently. So, tell me again: what are you really paying for? You would be better off investing a portion of your money in three different index ETFs (exchange-traded funds) that charge no upfront fees and have much lower management expenses (mutual funds often charge management fees of 1.5% or more per year on top of the initial upfront fee, as well as an annual 12b-1 fee of .25% split by the brokerage and advisor). Is it any wonder that, with all those fees, fund managers have difficulty beating the indices? You could divide your investment into three portions: one in the Dow Jones Industrials Index (DIA), one in the Standard & Poor's 500 Index (SPY), and the other in the Nasdaq 100 Index (QQQ). Each of these indexes will lead at one time or another, so holding some in each will keep you from missing a big move. Also, you can limit your losses because the three indexes are not perfectly correlated, meaning sometimes one will rise while one or more will fall.

Buying and holding index funds, in the beginning, is fine because you can be on autopilot while you accumulate enough to start buying individual stocks in meaningful numbers to provide the diversification necessary to reduce overall portfolio risk. If you start out with $10,000 and put it all into your favorite stock at the time, it could be great if that stock goes up, But if you choose poorly and the stock falls in value, your entire portfolio is at risk. Diversifying your portfolio across several stocks is preferable so that if one underperforms, it only affects a small portion of your portfolio. I think it best to wait until you can afford to buy similar-sized positions in at least eight stocks from eight different sectors. That provides a minimal level of diversification to lessen your risk exposure. Ideally, you should own at least 16 stocks, but more than 30 may be unnecessary to reduce risk to tolerable levels.

That may seem a lot to keep track of, but if you did your homework on each one before buying, an annual reevaluation of each stock is all that is necessary. You will want to make sure the business model has not changed in a negative way, and that management is still performing well. Generally, this is easy to determine by looking at the consistency of results on a year-over-year and quarterly basis. When revenue starts falling (except during a recession) while the revenue of its peers is rising, that is a red flag. If operating margins are falling without a resulting faster rise in revenue, then profits and cash flow will fall, another red flag. I will get into this area more later in the book.

Another benefit of buying index funds is that the dividends are automatically reinvested. This keeps investing simple when you are starting out. But be aware that not all stocks in index funds pay dividends, so your yields on investment will be inferior to what you could be achieving by holding quality individual stocks that pay a rising dividend.

The problem I have with investing in ETFs and index funds over the long term is that you are buying all the stock in the index: the good, the average, and the bad. The bad stocks will tend to hold your returns down, while the good ones will boost the overall returns. When investing for the long term, I prefer buying only above-average companies so my portfolio will not be hampered by holding underperforming stocks.

That is not to say that all good companies will outperform the market, especially over the short term. Even some of the best-quality companies can go through difficult times. Changes in management do not always work out for the better. But the best companies always find a way to right the ship and get back on track. That is what makes them quality companies.

You may not like fast food, but McDonalds (MCD) is a quality company. After a change in management a few years back, the company went through a disappointing period. That was a buying opportunity. Management was replaced by leaders with a better vision of how the company could improve growth and increase profitability, and it has done very well ever since. A similar thing happened at Procter and Gamble (PG). A successful CEO hand-picked his successor, but the results were terrible. The retired CEO came back and got the company back to growth and found a better replacement with a far superior vision of the company's future. It all worked out well. But, again, there was a buying opportunity when things went sour for a while. I could list a lot of similar situations, but I think you get the idea.

When a company has a proven track record, a culture that breeds success, and an unassailable moat that allows it to weather such storms and come out stronger, that is the definition of a quality company.

Now, most financial advisors will recommend that you buy mutual funds. Hopefully, you understand why by now. They make more money upfront when you buy a mutual fund than if you buy individual stocks. However, if you use a financial adviser to help you select and buy your stocks, manage your portfolio, etc., you are probably paying roughly 1% of your assets under management (AUM) for that service. That is okay if you need help early on, but once you have accumulated enough to fill out your portfolio to a good diversification level, you could take control of your portfolio and just add to the stocks you already own each year and save thousands of dollars. Those savings will help you achieve your next milestones faster. You should be at that point by the time you have a portfolio of $200,000. You could own 30 stocks with an average of almost $7,000 in each. And you would save $2,000 in fees each year.

It all may seem daunting when you first start investing, but it will get easier as time passes and you gain experience. That is why starting out by investing in index funds makes sense. It is like learning how to ride a bike with trainer wheels. But do not take the training wheels off until you are sure you are ready to manage on your own. If you take them off too soon and make mistakes, you may want to seek help again until you rebuild your confidence.

Interlude 4

The Booking Clerk

Jack Gsantner[8]

Jack was a former billing clerk for Union Pacific Railroad in Omaha, Nebraska. If you had met him, you would never have known from what he was wearing that he was a millionaire. After his wife died, he never remarried.

Jack was a saver, according to a close relative, due to his growing up during the recession. When he died, it appeared that Jack's entire estate consisted of his home, which was valued at $125,000. Then, other things of value were uncovered, like a pile of stock certificates and a deed to a townhouse in Arizona. Once the treasure hunt had concluded, it was estimated that at one point, Jack had owned as many as twenty rental properties and that his net worth was over $5 million.

Jack liked income-producing investments. He was patient. He held investments for the long term. Those are three important keys to building great wealth. Other keys are investing in companies or neighborhoods that you understand at bargain prices and always sticking with quality.

Jack never made a lot of money from his work, but he sure knew what to do with what little he had.

---

[8] More can be found about Jack at: https://elderlawnebraska.com/the-strange-case-of-jack-h-gsantner/

Part V:
Investing Decisions

Chapter 20:
How and Why I Sell Stocks

When and Why I might trim a position or two from my portfolio

There are two reasons that I might want to sell a stock position from my portfolio. The first is when the company management changes direction or the business model in a way that does not appear to be sustainable to me. This is something more than just a temporary setback of a quarter or two. In the case of McDonald's mentioned earlier, I held on. However, in the case of Procter and Gamble, I sold because the management was making changes that were too big and bad to ignore. But when the old CEO came back, I got back in. This should be obvious, but I do not want to exclude anything that could be useful to those just starting out. If the fundamental reason I bought the stock has changed, such as the moat has been washed away by technological advances creating easy entrance by competitors, I must reassess whether holding the position still makes sense. Often, in such a case, the answer is no. Thus, I will want to sell the stock and look for another investment with a more sustainable growth/income business model that is still intact.

The second reason is when I sense, for many reasons, that the market, and by extension, some of my positions, have reached overly high valuations. I will discuss the many reasons in a moment. But, for now, suffice it to say that when I feel that I could find a better investment for my money in terms of total return potential, I consider selling the position. The method, in this case, is to sell calls. In the first case, I will sell the position outright on a day when the stock exhibits some price strength (usually when the broader market is up and most stocks are lifted higher). In the second case, I will sell the calls when the stock is over its fair value by 50 percent or more and do so while the stock is still near its 52-week high. You would be surprised at how overvalued a stock can become.

The methods I use to liquidate a position

I want to provide two examples, one to explain each situation in which I decide to sell a position. The first example is Best Buy (NYSE: BBY), which I purchased on October 7, 2011. I had originally wanted the shares because of BBY's position as the leading electronics retailer after consolidation in the space and because of my firsthand experiences while shopping at three different BBY locations. I received some negative feedback after my original article that customer service in some areas had become less than desirable. I considered that to be more of a localized situation as my recent experiences had been superior.

Then something changed. On my next visit, all the highly knowledgeable employees that had made my shopping experience enjoyable suddenly disappeared. The employees who replaced them barely spoke English and were not as interested in helping me find what I needed. Instead, they were totally focused on selling me something along with some other things that I did not need. They were highly trained in selling but knew little about the products they were charged with selling. Fortunately for me, this happened in September 2013, when the price traded near $38 per share. I dumped my 200 shares on September 16th at $38.50.

69

One of the major reasons why I had bought stock in the company, excellent customer service, had changed dramatically. I was lucky to be shopping and having the experience when I did. Sure, the stock went up to over $43 per share in November of that year, two months after I had sold. But I felt no regret at the time. My decision was based upon the assumption that the company had decided to lower labor costs and try to increase dollars per sale at the expense of customer service. Management did not think it would be sacrificing so much in the customer experience, but, in the end, the result was horrific. Results disappointed, and the stock price fell back to a low of $22.15 in January 2014. I was not tempted to add back shares at that price. While I would have profited nicely if I had, the company had broken my faith, and I did not look back. Of course, the bigger future problem for BBY will be competing over the Internet with the likes of Amazon and some smaller electronics specialty sites. However, as I write this, Best Buy has again transformed itself, including better customer service, and it could find itself back on my buy list if the value becomes a bargain.

The second example is a company that I have held in my tax-deferred IRA account since 2006, with a cost basis of just over $30 per share. McCormick (NYSE: MKC) was one of my all-time favorite companies, but the stock, like many quality stocks in the current environment, became overvalued by my estimates. I really did not want to sell these shares because the company was still doing everything right, and the future remained bright. However, when the price of a stock gets to be overvalued by 50 percent or more, I like to sell calls above the current price. If the stock rallies and remains above my strike price, I end up having to sell the stock for 50 percent or more above what I consider to be fair value.

I believe that the growth prospects going forward will be lower, not only for MKC but for most multinational corporations, as growth in emerging markets is slowing and not likely to regain the levels of past decades in the foreseeable future. My estimated compound annual growth rate for MKC dividends was 6.6 percent. I plugged in the numbers and ended up with a fair value of $66.01 per share. By 2020, the stock had reached a split-adjusted price of over $100, and I was able to get out in the $90s (on 400 shares after the split). Not long ago, the price was languishing around $68, and the dividend had been cut. It does not matter whether I was smart or lucky; either way, I am glad I got out when I did.

Since the position was in my IRA account, I was not worried about tax consequences. I figured that if the position got called away, I would look for a better yield in another quality stock that has been beaten down more. That turned out well since the stock dropped, and the company revenues lost momentum.

I prefer to hold stocks forever, but sometimes, it does not make sense to do so. One event that will require the sale of a stock is when/if the company announces a cut to its dividend. Usually, I have already noticed a downturn in the results reported by the company for several quarters before this happened and am able to get out ahead of the cut. When a company cuts its dividend, it tells us that there is not enough free cash flow to pay out a rising dividend. It is better to face reality and get out than to hope for the company to right itself because a dividend cut usually leads to a big drop in the price of the stock.

Chapter 21:
Why I Buy Stocks with a
Long History of Increasing Dividends

A study I once read that covered the long-term returns of the S&P 500 index components had determined that over 40% of the total return from those stocks was historically generated by dividends and reinvesting that income back into stocks within the index. That study included all 500 component companies; the great companies, good ones, mediocre ones, and the outright terrible companies that eventually get dropped from the index. An individual investor can, with a little extra due diligence, do much better.

I prefer not to miss out on 40% of my potential total returns. There are plenty of high-quality companies that pay rising dividends to choose from that, over the long term, will provide the kind of retirement income you deserve.

The second reason (and the most important one) is that I like layering income streams, one on top of the other, building a future total income stream that I can live comfortably on without having to sell my underlying, income-producing assets. Remember, when you buy a dividend-paying stock today, 30 years from now, your dividend from that one stock could easily be more than 20% in each year of what you paid initially. That is an enormously powerful motivator for me. If people can just visualize that, it should be for them, too.

Imagine investing $10,000 in one or more stocks today with the understanding that when you retire, that same investment could be providing $2,000 of income to you every year for the rest of your life! Do that repeatedly throughout your working life, and your retirement income will keep growing every year, in inflation-adjusted dollars, instead of having your buying power decrease over time.

For example, I will use a company that has been relevant to investors for a long time because it has risen nicely over time since it became publicly traded in August of 1994: Amgen (AMGN). The company currently pays a dividend yield of 2.88% (June 2024). It has only paid a dividend for 12 years, but the dividend has increased an average of 9.6% over the past five years. That rate may slow down in the future, but I expect it to maintain a growth rate of at least 7% over the long term. By year 30, your dividend yield on the original investment would be 21.9%. If the rate of increase to the dividend averaged 8% per year, the yield on investment in year 30 would be 29%. So, for every $10,000 invested at this time (hypothetically), an investor could receive $2,900 per year, and that amount would keep growing faster than the rate of inflation for the rest of one's life. The power of compounding becomes enormous during retirement, just when you need it the most. But you need to start building that foundation today to get the greatest benefit later.

I want to offer another example of a company that could maintain good growth for several decades due to its drug pipeline, especially in weight loss: Ely Lilly (LLY). The dividend yield is only 0.73% now, but it has grown at a rate of 15% per year over the past five years. If (and this is a big IF) it can maintain that rate of growth for its dividend, the yield on the original investment would be 37.7% in year 30. I am not suggesting that the company will be able to do that, but the point is that the rate of growth is often more important than the original yield.

Once again, I want to reiterate that it is not how much money you have at retirement that creates financial security; it is the amount of annual income your investments produce for you year after year.

So, when the market goes down, and everyone is selling at the bottom out of fear that it could keep going down, you can ignore the balance of your portfolio and focus on how much income it is generating. If the income is more this year than it was last year, you are still on the right track. If you stick with quality companies, the balance will always rebound and be higher in the future, along with the income stream it produces.

The stock price of dividend-paying stocks usually keeps up with the increases in the dividend each year, at least over the long term. So, if you buy a company that pays a dividend yield of three percent and the company increases the dividend by seven percent a year, the stock will end up increasing in value by an average of about seven percent per year while you are also collecting the three percent dividend; total return equals ten percent per year.

There are several sources that list "dividend-paying stocks that raise their respective dividends consistently every year." Just type the phrase in quotes above into any search engine, and you will find what you need to get started.

Dividend Kings

Dividend Kings are companies that have increased their dividend for at least 50 consecutive years through all the recessions, wars, inflations, pandemics, etc. Many of these companies will often generate slower growth relative to the overall market, but over the long term, the stock price will usually keep pace with the growth in the dividend payout as long as revenue and earnings are also growing adequately to support strong coverage of the dividend. And remember: some of that growth comes from simple inflation every year as prices and profits rise to keep up.

To focus on the better-growing companies, I tend to look for companies that have consistent growth in revenue, earnings and increase dividends by an average of at least 6% per year. Of course, I also do some additional due diligence, as discussed elsewhere in this book. But that is my first cut, so to speak.

Dividend Aristocrats

Dividend Aristocrats are companies that have increased their dividend for at least 25 consecutive years through everything that goes wrong with the economy. This is a longer list with some very worthy candidates that still have many years of above-average growth ahead of them. Again, I use the same first-cut analysis to winnow the list before digging deeper into each company. Of course, the Dividend Kings will be on this list, just as the Kings and Aristocrats will be on the Achievers list mentioned below.

Analysis and selection are really a process of elimination. Once you get a list, you can load that list into stock analysis tools, such as Stock Rover (my favorite), and screen the group according to each of the criteria you use. Once you get used to using a stock screening tool, the entire process will be very simple and efficient. Screening allows you to determine which companies meet all the criteria you require with a click of the mouse (once you set up the screening parameters and save it). This makes the annual review process a breeze, too.

Dividend Achievers

Dividend Achievers are companies that have increased their dividend for at least 10 consecutive years. This list has some interesting companies that have made the switch from high growth to a more stable growth pattern but still have the potential to lead the markets. Apple (AAPL) is one such company on this list.

The same analysis and selection process applies once again. In total, over 350 stocks are included in the three lists above. Always be on the prowl to find the best one at any given time when preparing to add a stock to your portfolio. Pay less attention to the one-year target by any analyst and look for consistency coupled with current value based upon the Price to FCF ratio of 15 or less, or use a dividend discount model to look for the most undervalued company. Either method will get you to the one for which you are looking. I tend to use both just because I am extra cautious and like companies that look undervalued using both methods.

Chapter 22:
Consider the Tax Consequences of Investing

What I put into my taxable accounts

I will start off with an investment I have absolutely no intention of selling ever and that will have no capital gains: municipal bonds. These securities have long been a stalwart of retirees looking for federal tax-free income. These securities are also targeted by those in higher income brackets. Historically, municipal bonds have enjoyed an exceptionally low default rate averaging just 2.7 defaults per year from 1970-2009. During that 40-year span, only five general obligation [GO] bonds defaulted, amounting to only about seven percent of total municipal bond defaults. Most municipal bond defaults historically occurred in issues supporting healthcare and housing projects (73 percent of all defaults).

How times have changed! Since the Financial Crisis, we need to do more homework on selecting municipal bonds. The total number of municipal bonds rated by Moody's in 2011 was about 17,700. Even then, most municipal bonds were rated A3 or better by Moody's. By the end of 2013, Moody's was rating approximately 2,000 fewer municipal bond issues. The overall default rate had risen from .01 percent prior to 2007 to .03 percent, still an exceptionally low rate. However, a trend emerged, according to Moody.

Headlines covered many of the concerns about major municipal bond defaults like Harrisburg, PA; Stockton, CA; Jefferson County, AL; and Detroit, MI. Puerto Rico had its troubles, and both Chicago and the State of Illinois raised concerns in the headlines. I have some simple rules to avoid municipal bond defaults.

I avoid GO (General Obligation) issues in cities, counties, and states where pensions are funded below 75 percent. If you want to look up distressed pension plans of local governments, you can easily "Google" (search) for what you want to know. I searched for Pennsylvania (because I knew there were many problems in local pensions there) in 2013 and found a link to about 562 of the local municipality pension plans being underfunded by $7.7 billion. That equates to 46 percent of the locally administered pension plans in the state!

This does not include all underfunded plans, just the ones considered in distress. The point is that we need to be very selective when buying GO bonds and do a little due diligence.

I prefer revenue bonds backed by a sustainable stream of revenue, such as a toll road or airport. But even then, I take a long, hard look at the financial history and projected financials to make sure that revenues have been covering debt service obligations fully after operating expenses as well as fully funding the required sinking fund for the eventual debt repayment. That information should be available in a prospectus for the issue. You should also be able to get research reports and a prospectus from your brokerage, usually online. I only buy municipal bonds rated "A3" (by Moody's) or better and only when I can secure a yield of at least five percent per year to maturity.

Those are my rules. Adjust them as you see fit to suit your needs or make your own.

I do not plan to provide that much detail about each investment category, but I felt that municipal bonds tend to get ignored, so I thought it might be helpful to provide more information. I did not begin to buy municipal bonds until my mid-60s when I began looking for a solid yield with tax avoidance benefits.

Next, I also hold some stocks in taxable accounts. It depends upon where I have cash available (taxable or tax-deferred accounts) and what type of equity I am buying as to which account I use for the purchase. This is important because you can let several percentage points slip away to taxes unless you plan ahead.

Foreign stocks will go into my taxable account so that I can get either a refund of withheld taxes or a tax credit on my tax return. It all depends on the bilateral agreement between the U.S. and the country where the company is based.

High-quality domestic or foreign companies that tend to do better than the overall market in downturns and have a long history of increasing dividends with no dividend cuts can go into either account, depending on where I have cash available. I do not worry so much about the capital gains tax on these holdings because I intend to keep them forever. Dividend income is taxed at a low rate currently, but that could change. I tend to put more of these securities into my tax-deferred accounts because of the potential for the dividend and capital gains taxes to be increased in the future.

Something that too many investors forget to do is match losing positions against winning positions to avoid capital gains taxes when selling. I do not sell often, but it could be something to consider if I want to move positions from a taxable account to an IRA.

Occasionally, I have a position that goes negative early in my holding period. I can sell that stock along with another stock with a gain of comparable size relative to the unrealized loss to avoid the tax. Then, I can use the cash to contribute to my IRA. Assuming I still like both positions at the current price, I can buy the shares in my IRA, but not until after the 30-day wash period. It is inconvenient and possible to miss a small move in either stock, but it facilitates the movement of funds from taxable accounts to tax-deferred accounts. The catch is that you must still have enough earned income reported to the IRS to cover the contributions, which can sometimes be a problem for retirees. If the tax laws change and the tax on dividends increases too much, I plan to use this method to move some shares each year to tax-deferred accounts to lower my tax bill. For me, anything over a 20 percent tax rate on dividends will prompt some movement to my wife's or my Roth IRA accounts.

All rental real estate properties are held as taxable investments. One could put real estate into a Roth IRA, but the tax advantages are significant already without taking that step. The one time it can get expensive tax-wise is when one decides to sell a property. Well, another time is when the mortgage gets paid down, and the property is fully depreciated, but there is a way around paying the taxes. Admittedly, I have not yet done this, but one could enter a like-kind exchange to purchase another rental property of greater value but similar equity) and defer the capital gain.

An example would be to trade a single-family residential rental property for either a larger, more expensive single-family property or for a multi-family property of up to four units. More than four units may not be considered a like exchange, if I recall correctly, when I was looking into this a few years ago. The value of exchange is limited to the equity in each property. If the equity held by each party is equal, there would be no capital gain involved. One party is looking for current income, while the other (the buyer of the larger property) is looking for future income and, thus, more current leverage and tax deductions. This strategy is worthwhile for those who get started in real estate early in life and get to the point where too much positive taxable income is being generated from a property.

One can also trade one residential property for two or three single-family residences, each with lower equity built up so that the total equity on both sides of the trade is nearly equal. However, this requires more time to inspect and verify expenses for each property and more time to manage. But, it is an option for those interested in sticking to single-family properties.

Of course, I also hold all my precious metals in taxable form. It can be added to an IRA, but because there is no income, I do not choose to go that route.

Finally, I also hold cash and BIL ETF shares in both types of accounts. Unfortunately, interest income in a taxable account is taxed as regular income. My wife also likes to buy CDs (certificates of deposit) at the credit union each month when we have at least $1,000 extra. That income also gets taxed as regular income, but at least I do not need to pay withholding (Social Security, Medicare, and Medicaid) tax on it.

What I put into my tax-deferred accounts

My tax-deferred account may hold some corporate bonds of companies that I expect to be around long after I am gone. Currently, I do not hold any corporate or government bonds (other than BIL ETF). When I do buy bonds (and I will again when interest rates are higher – I prefer a rate of seven percent or higher), I stick with investment-grade bonds issued by companies that I know and understand. I prefer rates much higher than have been available since before 2008. My cut-off is seven percent. I realize that such a high rate may seem crazy in the current interest rate environment, but that should explain why I do not have any right now. Once again, I will be patient and pick up the bargains when availability improves. I do not expect that to occur unless there is a general financial crisis or inflation rears its head in a big way again.

The reason I hold bonds, especially long-term bonds, in my tax-deferred accounts is that otherwise, the income is taxed at my personal income tax rate. This way, I do not pay taxes on the interest income until I withdraw money from my account (and only if it is in my traditional IRA and not Roth since the Roth withdrawals are tax-free).

As to inflation relative to equity values, a little is good for stocks, but too much is a killer. The same holds true for bonds. Sustained inflation above five percent will cause long-term interest rates to rise to levels where investors may be able to capture quality issues yielding eight percent or more. Locking in a long-term yield above eight percent is something that every investor needs to take advantage of. I do not expect such an environment for several more years here in the U.S. But I do believe we will see it again before too long since the deflationary pressures following the financial crisis have lifted as the millennial generation hits its earnings potential stride sometime in the late-2020s. If I am still writing when the time comes, I will be sure to provide my viewpoint about when interest rates are hitting a peak. The Fed stops raising the discount rate and inflation begins to taper slightly when the peak has been reached. I may not catch the top, but I will be loading up shortly after it is achieved. Even if rates go a little higher, I will refrain from crying tears of regret as I will have my eight percent or more each year to console me.

Treasuries fit the same profile as corporate bonds, but I prefer corporate bonds over Treasury bonds for the higher yield, assuming the relationship remains in the future. I doubt that we will see another period like the one we had in the 80s when 30-year Treasury bonds hit 15 percent. But with all the debt around, who knows? If Treasuries were to get near that level again, I would need to reconsider and weigh the options. The one thing that may keep me out of long-term Treasuries is the possibility that the U.S. dollar could lose its reserve currency status. If that happens, combined with the mounting federal debt level, the dollar could lose value relative to other major currencies, and U.S. Treasury securities could fall in price as a result. Just something to keep in mind and watch for in the years ahead.

Foreign sovereign bonds are an asset I would only hold in my tax-deferred account. The reason is twofold: while I might be giving up some withholding of interest in some cases, the relative currency values [FX] and current income tax issue outweigh that consideration, in my opinion. Of course, I would want to do my due diligence on the withholding issue to make sure I was not stepping into something egregiously unfair first. However, consider the impact of FX on Japanese bonds. As the US dollar (USD) increases in value, the value of a yen-denominated bond falls precipitously on a USD basis. The FX part of the equation can be the biggest benefit of investing in foreign bonds. I also do not like to pay income tax on interest if I can avoid it.

Foreign sovereign bonds issued by creditworthy nations can be a boon to your portfolio for a couple of reasons. First, you may be able to earn a higher interest rate on the bonds as many countries historically have held interest rates higher than the U.S. That is because of the implied safety of the U.S. sovereign bonds relative to most other sovereign bonds. Another reason is that it adds more diversity to a portfolio since there is generally less correlation between US bonds and equities relative to foreign bonds. Finally, and this is my favorite part, the FX gains can be huge. Be careful, though; the time to buy foreign sovereign bonds is when the USD is historically strong relative to most other currencies. When the USD hits a high and begins to fall again relative to other currencies, it behooves us to seek out the countries with both higher yields and faster-growing economies (without high debt burdens) for potentially outsized future gains. If interest rates are high and beginning to fall in that country, then they can earn three ways: gains from the principal value of bonds rising as interest rates fall, locked in high interest rates, and gains from changes in relative values of currencies. Such circumstances do not come often, but when it happens, you want to be in the mix with at least a small portion of your portfolio.

Finally, I only hold these securities in my tax-deferred accounts because of the volatility of the FX. These are investments that may do well for several years at a time, but there is a cyclicality to investing in this area, and one must be ready to sell when the environment begins to change. Because I expect to be taking gains and not holding to maturity, I like to avoid taxes, especially on the gains that can be substantial.

Stocks of companies that I plan to hold forever, those quality companies that have an established record of growing revenues, earnings, and dividends (especially dividends) can usually go into my tax-deferred accounts. As I pointed out in the previous section, it depends on where I have the cash available when I spot a great bargain. I prefer to keep these issues in my tax-deferred accounts for tax reasons even though the tax rate on dividends is low now; the rate tends to move over time, so I prefer to keep the income out of reach of our dear Uncle Sam.

Some folks like to keep royalty trusts and limited partnership units in a taxable account to avoid going over the limit on "income earned from other than normal business." There is a limit on what can be earned in a tax-deferred account per individual in a year without becoming taxable from such investments. An investor needs to keep this in mind and look at previous K-1 schedules from a company (usually a limited partnership or trust) to get a sense of how much income is likely to be distributed for each share annually that falls into this category. It does not take long to make that investigation and do the math. The information can usually be found under the "Investors" tab on the company website, such as "tax treatment of distributions."

I do not own any such shares/units presently but have in the past. I did very well by owning Canadian royalty trusts before the government north of the border decided to change how distributions were taxed. I sold as soon as I read what was being proposed and did not wait for the law to be voted on. It hurt because my monthly distributions from those units were about $2,000 at the time. The nice part was that a portion of each distribution was considered a return of capital and free from taxes. The distributions were also considered qualified dividends then. I held those units in my taxable account because the effective rate on the distributions was only about ten percent. But then, I do my own taxes, so I do not have to pay an accountant to file each K-1 for me.

That can cost a pretty penny (or about $100 or more per K-1). So, if you only want to own a hundred units and you have your taxes prepared professionally, you may save money by either holding the units in a tax-deferred account or just telling the preparer to declare the full amount as taxable income instead of filing the K-1. You can find examples of how to file a K-1 by searching the Internet. If annual distributions from a single K-1 total less than $1,000, it might be cheaper to pay tax on the whole amount instead of paying your preparer.

As to the question of where I should hold this type of security, the answer lies in the following questions: How much of the asset do you want to own? What is your tax rate? Do you pay a preparer to file your taxes? Then, do the math. It seems complicated, but it really is not. And the yields can be particularly good. The point is that an investor could own these types of securities in either taxable or tax-deferred accounts. It depends on the answers and the math to decide which is better.

How I deal with foreign stock dividend withholding

In a nutshell, it depends upon the bilateral tax treaty between the U.S. and the nation in which the foreign company resides. Here is a link to the IRS page

https://www.irs.gov/businesses/internationalbusinesses/united-states-income-tax-treaties-a-to-z, United States Tax Treaties – A to Z) with links to all the current tax treaties with foreign governments. I apologize that the treaty language is in legal jargon and may be difficult to understand. When you click on a country, it brings up the original treaty document. Scroll down to the articles list and find articles that cover dividends (usually article ten) or royalties (usually article 12) if you are considering a royalty trust). First, look for the rate at which the countries have agreed to tax dividends, often 15 percent, but may be higher. Then, look within the section titled "Relief from double taxation" for information about refunds and/or tax credits. Some developed countries have a form to apply for a refund of withheld taxes. Often, the best you can hope for is to report the withheld tax on your filed return and then receive a tax credit equal to the difference between what you paid and what you would have paid if the dividend had been paid and taxed in the U.S. When the tax withheld is below what our tax rate is, you may find you owe additional taxes to the U.S if held in a taxable account. What you want to be certain of is that you will be able to avoid being taxed at more than the prevailing U.S. rate.

In the end, by holding such securities in a taxable account, you can keep the tax rate down to the dividend tax rate in the U.S. One thing to remember is that if the tax rate is lower than the U.S. tax rate, you can keep more of your dividend by owning it in a tax-deferred account. Do your homework and save some money from the tax man every year you hold the stock. If you are a long-term investor and buy a high-quality dividend-paying foreign stock, the savings could add up over the decades to a nice sum.

Summary

This chapter is intended as an explanation of what I have learned from my own experience and how I plan to avoid taxes. In some cases, I find that there is no clear-cut definition of what is best without doing a little homework. I am not a tax expert, nor is any of the information included in this article meant to be advice other than to provide some perspective for other investors.

Chapter 23:
Don't Fight the Fed!

That is an old saying, and it holds true most of the time. The Federal Reserve Bank (and, more specifically, the FOMC (Federal Open Market Committee) can exert a lot of pressure on stock trends. There are a couple of reasons for that.

Cost of Capital

First, when the FOMC decides to raise interest rates, it increases the cost of capital (borrowing) for many companies, especially those in capital-intensive industries such as transportation, utilities, retail, real estate, wholesale distribution, etc.

For example, in transportation, such as truck freight companies, trucks, and trailers are expensive to buy and maintain. They also wear out and must be replaced. Many such companies also require large distribution facilities to break down and consolidate loads from short-haul origins to long-haul destinations and then for delivery. Those operations also require lots of specialized equipment that is expensive to buy and maintain. It also wears out and must be replaced.

Think about the airline industry. They either must buy or lease planes that cost millions of dollars, then must maintain them and fuel them for each flight. Then there is the baggage handling equipment, etc. All these things require capital investments, wear out over time, and must be replaced periodically.

The same holds true for shipping companies and railroads. But the railroads must also build and maintain hundreds, if not thousands, of miles of track. Lots of capital expenditures every year.

As interest rates rise, so does the cost of borrowing money. Many companies, like the utilities, must borrow money to maintain and expand operations constantly to keep up with rising demand.

The cost of capital also discourages acquisitions and mergers because borrowing becomes too expensive. So, companies that need to be acquired must wait for a lower-cost environment, and buyers decide to wait as well.

The bottom line is that higher or rising costs of capital can mute investment and slow growth in the economy and, by extension, the stock market. So, it is generally not wise to invest in stocks as interest rates are rising.

However, the stock market is forward-looking, which means that when interest rates fall, the opposite is expected to happen, and stocks tend to rise in such an environment. That is why, even when the economy is contracting and falling into recession, stocks will begin to trend higher before the economic conditions improve.

This is one of the many reasons that trying to time the market is so difficult. Emotionally, it is very difficult to invest in stocks when the economy is performing at its worst. Once most people look at their depleted balances of stock portfolios, they tend to sell to avoid further losses. But a lot of the selling happens at or near the very bottom. This is called the capitulation phase. It often takes the form of a big day down (like 1,000 points on the DJIA) early, with a bounce to end the day at nearly flat. That is often the best buying opportunity that will come along for several years if it happens. Capitulation is not always that abrupt, but when it is, we, as investors, need to suck it up and jump in while everyone else is getting out. This is especially true when the market is already down by 30% or more.

The opposite is also true in the case of the market making new all-time highs. Most investors catch the FOMO (Fear of Missing Out) bug and buy at what may be the worst possible time when most stocks are wildly overvalued. These are the reasons that the average investor experiences a gain of around 3% over a lifetime, even when the market averages 7-9%. Do not let yourself be an average investor.

The Discount Rate for Valuing Stocks

The discount rate (not to be confused with the Fed discount rate that it charges banks for overnight borrowing) is the "expected" long-term cost of capital and is used to value companies by discounting future expected cash flows to a present value for the company.

High-growth companies, like those found in the tech sector or communications, trade at higher valuations when interest rates are extremely low and tend to trade at less high valuations when interest rates rise.

Companies with low capital requirements and high profit margins are generally categorized as growth stocks. The "Magnificent Seven" stocks (Apple, Alphabet, Microsoft, Tesla, Meta, Nvidia, and Amazon) fall into this category, apart from Amazon and Tesla, which are more capital-intensive. This is why the Nasdaq (QQQ) Index fell from around 15,900 at the end of 2021 to less than 10,500 near the end of 2022. For those keeping score at home, that represents a drop of over 33% in one year. That all happened because the Federal Reserve kept raising interest rates aggressively. However, the markets rebounded in 2023 even though the Fed did not signal that it would pause raising interest rates until the final quarter of that year.

The move up was one that had its ups and downs, but it ended the year strongly because market participants became convinced that the Fed would soon begin to cut rates, giving rise to higher future valuations.

It is also important to note that "the market" was led by the Magnificent Seven stocks, which accounted for most of the increased valuations of all three Indexes. This is why, when starting out, it is often best to keep your money invested in the no-load index ETFs (ExchangeTraded Funds). You can avoid the emotions, knowing that the markets will do better than most investors over the long term, and you will not miss the big bounces off intermediate or long-term bottoms that often occur. Once an investor has accumulated $100,000 or more, it should be time to start buying individual stocks that pay rising dividends to build future streams of income. But that is just my rule of thumb to guide young investors because it can be difficult to create a portfolio that is diversified enough to keep risk at an acceptable level with much less than that amount. We always need to manage risk. And one way to manage risk is to not go against the fiscal policies of the Fed!

Which Means

When interest rates are rising, do not buy stocks; when interest rates are falling, do buy stocks, especially after a big drop in stock prices or well into a recession. The market (stocks) usually bottoms before the economy does.

Interlude 5

F.I.R.E.

While I was researching for real stories of ordinary people with average jobs who accumulated millions before they passed, I came across an intriguing group of people who have decided to save as much as possible early in life to enable them to retire by their early 40s, if not before. It is called FIRE[9]

or Financial Independence, Retire Early.

The concept of financial independence does not necessarily mean that they want to spend the rest of their lives traveling or playing golf. It means that they no longer need to work at a job they do not enjoy. It means that they can work at whatever they are passionate about without worrying about how to pay bills each month.

Barney Whiter[10]

The story I found was about a guy, Barney Whiter, who had a difficult childhood during which his parents had bought a big house with a huge mortgage and were living the life they enjoyed. They rarely denied themselves anything if they wanted it, whether it was an expensive vacation, a new car, a nice dinner out, new furniture, landscaping, etc. Everything was fine while the economy was strong. But when a recession hit and one of them lost their job, they realized that they were overextended and did not have enough savings to bridge the difficult times. That caused a lot of headaches, hardships and yelling.

As the boy grew into a man and entered the workforce, he decided that he would not be anything like his parents. He started saving as much as he could and thought carefully about every purchase, denying himself luxuries or frivolous things. He bought only what he needed to maintain his frugal but comfortable lifestyle. In short, he lived within his means, much like all the others that I have introduced in the interludes.

He retired at the age of 43.

9 https://www.businessinsider.com/personal-finance/financial-independence-retire-early
10 https://www.bbc.com/worklife/article/20181101-fire-the-movement-to-live-frugally-and-retire-decades-early

Part VI:
Be Reasonable with Expectations

Chapter 24:
Learning from Successes
and Failures

I have had successes and failures. We all do or will over a lifetime. The trick is to limit the failures and let the successes run. Knowing what to avoid is more important than knowing what to go after. You will make mistakes. The question to ask yourself is if you will repeat the same mistakes. Because that is exactly what most individual investors do. As I have mentioned before, most small investors jump out near the bottom and jump back in near the top of market moves. They get out when they should be doubling down and get in when they believe the coast is all clear after waiting too long to pull the trigger. I still wait too long sometimes and miss a good portion of a move I have identified in advance. It is only human nature to be overly cautious when a stock or the broad market is falling.

The key is to learn from your mistakes and not repeat them. When I told my friends to buy long-term, zero-coupon treasury bonds to fund their unborn baby's college education, I should have done the same thing, but I did not pull the trigger (buy) when I knew full well that it was a sound investment. I was just beginning to invest and had yet to develop rules to help me know when to engage and when to stay on the sidelines in cash while waiting for a better opportunity (plus, my wife and I had just bought our first house together and used much of our savings for furnishings and updates to the new property). At that point, I did not really understand what constituted a good investment opportunity, especially one that might not come again in my lifetime. Now that I have lived most of my life, I know full well what is special and what is merely average. That is the learning process. I hope this book will help readers shorten their learning curve so that they learn faster from mistakes and what to avoid to generate better results earlier in life than I did.

Warren Buffett, one of the greatest investors of all time, accumulates large amounts of cash repeatedly, especially when stocks have been trending higher for multiple years. He knows that through his patience, he will eventually find a great many wonderful bargains. He learned this lesson from the mistakes he made early in his investing career. He continually got better until he found the right combination of analysis tools and techniques that worked well consistently. He has not strayed from those proven methods for decades, and he is still winning!

One of my favorite quotes from Buffett: "Rule number 1: Don't lose money. Rule number 2: Don't forget rule number 1."

He has learned how to avoid big losses by using cash flow analysis and sticking with investing in companies that generate plenty of free cash flow, maintain a competitive advantage within their respective industries, and cultivate a culture that consistently produces growth.

Knowing when to buy is important, but knowing when to sell maybe even more important. In most cases, assuming one has chosen well, selling may never be necessary. But, when it is necessary, it is crucial to not ignore the signs of a business that is making bad decisions.

When there is stable leadership, and it sticks to what has worked for decades, there is not much to worry about. But when a new management team takes over, we need to keep a closer watch on their decisions. It may be an improvement, or it may lead to disaster.

When a company changes its business model in significant ways, it is time to watch closely. The key ratios to watch are margins: operating margin and net margin. If either of these ratios begins to fall, it may be time to move on to better opportunities.

But when investing for future dividend income, do not be too hasty to sell a quality company. Several companies have stumbled temporarily but turned things around to get back on track. McDonalds (MCD) did it. Procter & Gamble (PG) did it. Apple (AAPL) did it, too. There are many other examples, but I hope you get the point. When a company can keep raising its dividend through recessions, it may be wise to stick with it longer term.

Be Reasonable

Please do not create a plan that is more likely to fail than succeed. This is not a sprint (though you might like it to be); it is a marathon. Plan to meet the average returns of the market over the last two decades. If you exceed your plan, you can retire earlier than planned.

If you expect to beat the market every year, you will be prone to make more mistakes by swinging for the home runs instead of building consistent growth that can be relied upon. When you set the bar too high, it is only natural to buy companies that appear to have a lot of potential growth. The problem is that a lot of growth companies fizzle out and end up in bankruptcy, especially the small start-up businesses with a lot of hype. I know. I went down that path and made my share of dumb mistakes.

It is far better to create reasonable, achievable goals and exceed them rather than create goals that set you up for failure. Sticking with quality means focusing on large, proven companies that may not be able to grow rapidly every year. Companies that generate plenty of free cash flow have more flexibility when the economy contracts. Small companies get gobbled up by their larger competitors, giving those goliaths more growth potential. Big companies can afford to buy growth; small companies cannot. Big companies consolidate their industries during challenging times, while small companies either go out of business or get bought out for pennies on the dollar.

Stick with quality!

Chapter 25:
Start with a Goal that is Achievable
to Retire Comfortably

Creating my son's first plan

We started off talking about his horizon, which is a difficult concept to grasp right out of college. At the time, being single and focused on getting started off on the right foot, we stuck to what was important to him. He wanted to retire by age 60 and knew that if he did not start planning and saving early, his chances could be less than desirable. I may have had a hand in that.

He is also aware of how inflation requires him to need more nominal income in retirement and that he will, because of advances in medical technology, probably live longer and need sustainable income streams that will keep him ahead of inflation after retirement. He believed that having the equivalent of $50,000 in annual income (in 2011 dollars) would be sufficient to retire. He was also keen on a career in the Air Force as an intelligence officer. So, that was where we started.

First, we looked up the officer pay schedule on airforce.com, which lists the starting pay and in-grade increases for years of service. He would start at $33,941 in his first year as a second lieutenant. His cousin is a major after serving ten years, and a couple of my friends retired after twenty and thirty years of service, respectfully at the ranks of lieutenant colonel and colonel, each having spent more than five years in grade at the time of retirement. With that information and a reasonable assessment of my son's intelligence, attitude, and work habits, we made some assumptions about how his career would progress. Obviously, this is more predictable than most careers are likely to be, but it is an effective way to start the process.

It seems apparent from both the experience of people we know and the pay schedule that the Air Force does not expect an officer to remain below the grade of captain for more than five years. It also appears that a promotion to major should happen within the first twelve years. If the officer is hard-working, learns fast, and evolves into a valuable asset (which is what my son intended), one could expect to be a lieutenant colonel by year 15 and a full colonel sometime around year 22. After that point, we assumed he would not make it to the general level, so the expected salary at the time of his retirement would be $126,688 before inflation. His income would increase approximately 4.3% per year, from $33,941 to $126,688 (before inflation) over 30 years.

Formula = $((33941/126688)$ ^ $(1/30))$-1

However, we know that the pay schedule gets updated regularly to account for inflation, so we assumed an average of two percent annual adjustment. That would create a six percent annual compound rate of growth in income (2% for inflation and a 4% annual rise in income), and we end up with a final annual pay of about $183,906 per year 30 years from now. That may sound a lot better than it will feel.

We assumed that he would make the maximum contribution (ten percent) to his 401K plan (Thrift Savings Plan in federal government parlance) right from the start and that the Air Force would make a five percent matching contribution. We also assumed that the maximum contribution threshold would be indexed to allow him to not exceed the maximum amount allowable by law. In the end, assuming a cautious but flexible allocation that would result in a six percent compound annual rate of return, he would end up with $593,952 at the end of his 30-year career.

At that point, he would retire from the Air Force and seek a better-paying position in a private firm for the next ten years. He changed his mind about retiring at 60 once I explained that he may need to work in the private sector for ten years (to record 40 quarters of deductions) to be eligible for social security. With that in mind, we made the first adjustment, extending his expected working career by two years. When he is approaching retirement, he will decide whether social security benefits will be worth the additional effort. Extending his retirement savings into the new 401K plan, making the maximum contribution allowed by the employer, and assuming a continued five percent matching contribution while, at the same time, allowing the Air Force plan to continue to grow until he retires completely, we estimated that his total savings in the two plans would aggregate to a total of $1,587,338 by the time he reaches age 62.

Notice what happened over the last twelve years; without changing the rate of growth and by merely continuing to contribute the same percentage of a gradually rising income, the total increased by 167 percent from just under $600,000 to almost $1.6 million! That is the power of compound interest (growth) over time. Like magic, it gets better and better the longer you let it grow.

Next, we assumed that he would begin putting the maximum allowed contribution into an IRA at the end of his first year in the Air Force, or $5,500. We assumed a slightly more aggressive allocation to achieve an annual compound rate of return of eight percent. We did not make any assumptions about inflation or future increases to the maximum allowable contributions. Thus, this should be a conservative estimate. If he is consistent in contributing the maximum amount each year until age 62, when he plans to retire, we estimate that his IRA(s) should have a total of $1,494,117 accumulated.

As I pointed out in the previous installment, he plans to contribute initially to a Roth IRA while his income tax rate is still below 30 percent. At the point at which his incremental tax rate (combined for federal and state) hits 30 percent, he will switch his contributions to a traditional IRA to save on taxes if he feels he needs the relief to accommodate his lifestyle.

However, we also discussed that his income will be high enough in retirement, and his income tax rate may be more than 30 percent. One never knows what will happen to income tax rates in the future, so having as much tax-free income as possible is a good thing to plan for. To refresh the reader: Withdrawals from a Roth IRA after reaching retirement age are tax-free; withdrawals from a traditional IRA are fully taxed as earned income at the prevailing rate.

The thing to remember is that we are trying to create multiple streams of future income. So far, we have developed two future sources of income from savings. But wait! There is more! We assumed that he would not be able to save much in a taxable account during the first 17 years. Why? Well, he will need transportation and entertainment, and who knows, but he might even get married and have children. Then there is the house, another car (or a van/SUV), savings for the kids' college expenses, and all the extra expenses that accrue to a family with children. He will be saving in a taxable account, but I explained to him that he might not be able to hold onto much of it for quite a few years. There will be a down payment for car(s) and car payments, a down payment for a house and the additional maintenance expenses, and family vacations can be expensive (four people usually cost four times as much as one). It will be hard, but eventually, his income (and that of his wife if she works) will grow enough to allow for additional savings that can be targeted for retirement.

One other item that we discussed is that he needs to build a savings account as a buffer for emergencies. If he gets laid off or his wife does and there is a need to meet expenses while searching for employment, he will need to have an emergency fund to draw from. My wife and I have tried to keep the equivalent of six months of living expenses in our emergency savings account. We have needed it several times for things like moving, a new HVAC system for the house, a new roof, a new appliance, etc. It gets drawn down, and then we build it back up again. After talking it through, my son understood the need for an emergency savings account. We decided, after some negotiation, that he might be able to begin saving for retirement in a taxable account in about 18 years. He hopes to get there sooner, but we agreed to 18 years for the plan. So, he will be saving in that taxable account for 24 years before retirement, and we assumed an annual compound rate of growth of seven percent to allow for paying taxes on the dividends, interest, and gains when necessary.

His plan calls for him to save $5,000 in the first year and then increase the savings by $1,000 each year ($6,000 in year two, etc.) until he reaches $10,000 per year. He plans to continue to save $10,000 per year until retirement. We estimate that he should accumulate $506,565 by age 62 in his taxable account. His total savings from all three sources (401K, IRAs, and taxable savings) should be $3,448,769.

Future income streams

After concluding his savings plans, we moved on to identifying all future streams of income for retirement. The Air Force has a generous retirement plan. I am not certain, but I believe it pays about two percent per year of service time on the average of the high three years of salary. We estimated that the average of his last three years of income from the Air Force would be about $180,000. Thus, two percent times 30 years of service is 60 percent of that amount to calculate his annual pension. That results in a first-year pension of about $108,000 that he could begin to draw at age 52. We assumed an annual average of two percent cost of living adjustment until his death. If I am wrong and the Air Force has adjusted the pension to be one percent of the high three-year average, then his pension would be half as much. Still, it is just one stream of future income. There are more.

The second potential stream of income would be social security. This one is tough to estimate because we assume that adjustments will need to be made to the plan and benefits (later age requirement and reduced benefit). So, we tried to be conservative and estimated that he would be eligible for $18,000 of annual benefits in today's dollars and that he would not be able to begin receiving benefits until he reached 65 years of age. We also assumed that over that time, the cost-of-living adjustment would average two percent. At age 65, he could collect $41,350 (adjusted for inflation), and that amount would increase to $55,652 by age 80. That makes two income streams so far.

Now, we need to look at the retirement accounts for additional income when needed. The first one we will look at is the taxable account since it does not continue to accumulate on a tax-deferred basis like

IRAs.

My son would probably roll over his 401K savings from the Air Force (or other employer) into a traditional IRA account. Whether he rolls his private employer 401K over into a traditional or Roth IRA account will depend on the options he has when he begins his employment. If they offer a Roth 401K, he may go that route. Whatever the case, he will likely roll over each account to an IRA of similar tax treatment. Likewise, which account he decides to draw from will depend on his marginal tax rate during retirement each year.

The Roth IRA income will be tax-free. It went in after tax, and as it comes out, there are no taxes owed (unless Congress decides to change the rules). The withdrawals from the traditional IRAs will be fully taxed as earned income. The taxes were only deferred. None of the savings in the traditional IRAs will have had any taxes paid until the withdrawals begin.

We decided, for simplicity, to combine the 401K and IRA accounts into one stream and label it retirement savings income. He will take what he needs from whichever account makes the most sense to him at the time of withdrawal. Of course, there is a required minimum withdrawal that he will need to make from the traditional account(s) once he turns 73, so the IRS will have its say in at least part of the decision.

We assumed that he would have at least a six percent annual return from those accounts, including dividends and interest, and that income would increase each year. We also assumed that there would be some appreciation but that he would be investing very conservatively (read: mostly fixed income), so we also assumed that he could take out three percent each year and that he could increase his withdrawal by two percent per year. Our reasoning is that at such a low rate, he should not need to draw down the principal, making his savings last indefinitely. He has no idea how long he will live! If he begins withdrawals at age 62, he could add a third retirement income stream of $90,278 per year.

Adding the incomes together, we get a total of $224,572 per year. If we adjust for an average rate of inflation of three percent, that would equal about $70,909 in today's dollars, more than his goal. That is good because it is always more realistic to aim a little high and hope you come close. If he wanted, he could simply use only $158,351 in his first year of retirement and reinvest the rest. That is how much $50,000 would equal at a three percent average annual rate of inflation.

Now, if I was wrong about the Air Force pension plan and his income would be calculated at the one percent rate instead of two percent, then his income in his first year of retirement would be $157,425 in year one. Funny how that is less than six-tenths of one percent from his original goal.

Twelve years later, finds my son not in the Air Force but working for a private company with a good salary as a programmer. He started saving immediately, but at a little lower level initially. However, he has been able to increase his savings and is now back on schedule to meet his financial goals. All's well that ends well.

Summary

The point of this exercise is that a well-defined plan, consistent execution, and reasonable goals can work for most people, resulting in financial security. Obviously, there are setbacks, and no plan will work perfectly, but as shown here, even if he fell short of his goals and got behind his milestone targets, my son would still end up in decent shape. If he had no plan and started later in life, as most people do, he would not come close to achieving the wherewithal to retire as comfortably. Everyone will have different long-term objectives and goals. Thus, everyone needs to create a plan that is personalized and can help them achieve those goals. A person who has lesser ambition and expectations will, nonetheless, need a plan to be able to retire at their own level of comfort. It will not be any easier just because someone needs less to make them happy. No plan, haphazard savings, or swinging for the fence with every investment are all sure-fire ways to end up with less than one needs.

Chapter 26:
Analyzing the Financial Statements

My intent is to keep this as simple as possible because most people do not have time to do detailed analyses of multiple companies on a regular basis. So, with that in mind, I will stick to those items that I have found to be the most helpful. In a later chapter, I will include a list and description of the tools I use to create shortcuts for most of the analysis. For now, I will cover just the basics.

Income Statement

The first thing investors need to understand is earnings can be manipulated by management. The second thing investors need to understand is that quarterly earnings reports are hard to compare from one company to another because companies rarely use GAAP (Generally Accepted Accounting Principles) in press releases, and each company can apply a variety of adjustments to GAAP to arrive at their desired results.

So, I generally look at trends within the income statement that matter. Yes, I do look at net income (but I take it with a grain of salt) for consistent growth, but I always ignore reported income and look only at GAAP income (which can be found on the SEC platform called EDGAR as well as from the tools I use). GAAP income can still be manipulated, but it is closer to reality, and at least it makes it easier to compare competitors because they must all follow the same reporting rules under GAAP. I also look at the trend in operating income for consistent growth.

But my real focus is on margins, both operating and net. Of course, these can be manipulated, as well, but it is the trend at which I look. Margins do not need to grow over time (it is nice if they do), but it can be a red flag if margins are declining. If revenue increases and margins remain static, the result is increased income (unless management does not control non-operating expenses).

Finally, I would like to see consistent growth in revenue.

Balance Sheet

The balance sheet tells us whether the company has flexibility in its capital allocation. Too much debt can paint management into a corner and create a survival culture. I want to own companies that have the flexibility to allocate capital in the best way to create sustainable growth.

The balance sheet ratios I look at include total debt to assets, debt to equity, current ratio, and goodwill as a percentage of total assets. I will discuss each ratio below and explain what to look for with each.

Total debt to assets should be below 50% in most instances, depending on the industry. The closer this ratio is to 1.0, the less flexibility management will have in its capital allocation decisions, and the more reliant the company is on debt to maintain operations.

Debt to equity is similar in that the lower it is, the better. If a company has more debt than equity, it is probably borrowing money constantly just to stay alive. Equity is essentially the accumulation of profits the company has built up over its entire existence. Equity should be rising yearly. If it falls, the company could be headed to bankruptcy.

The current ratio is merely a check on the short-term solvency of the company. It is calculated by subtracting the current liabilities (including the short-term portion of debt) from the current assets. As long as the company is consistently maintaining a current ratio above 1.0, it remains solvent and should be able to pay its bills over the coming year.

Goodwill, expressed as a percentage of total assets, is a measure of how much a company has overpaid in the past for one or more acquisitions. If goodwill is greater than 50% of assets, the company really has a limited capacity to raise funds by issuing debt. Once again, this limits the flexibility of management's ability to allocate capital and could hinder future growth.

Cash Flow Statement

For me, this is where the rubber meets the road. Cash is cash and is much more difficult to manipulate than income. That makes it a much more reliable measure of a company's true health.

I want to start with my definition of FCF (Free Cash Flow):

Net Income + Depreciation + Amortization – Net Capital Expenditures.

This is much simpler than the contemporary definition of FCF, which includes changes to balance sheet items and other items that are transitory in nature and cannot be sustained over the long term. I also use GAAP (Generally Accepted Accounting Principles) net income rather than adjusted net income because it makes comparing companies simpler because there is only one set of rules defining net income that way. This calculation of FCF was first introduced by the founder of Value Line Investment Survey (a tool I have used for years), Arnold Bernhard. It just makes sense to me to capture only those elements that are sustainable year after year and less vulnerable to temporary management adjustments.

FCF is what is left over after all expenses are paid, including taxes and interest on debt, but before dividends are issued to shareholders. This represents what management can use for returning capital to shareholders, future growth through acquisitions, or for research and development to generate growth internally beyond the maintenance of current operations.

Those companies that consistently generate substantial amounts of FCF have greater flexibility in capital allocation because they have more capital to allocate. Efficient capital allocation, combined with innovation and sound execution, creates an environment capable of market-beating growth. That, combined with consistently superior results over at least five consecutive years, is what I define as a company with high-quality traits. Those are the companies I want to own for the long term, especially if those companies pay above-average yielding dividends that grow by at least 6% every year. And that, my fellow investors, is what powers wealth accumulation through compounding.

Specifically, I look for companies that generate stable or growing FCF as a percentage of revenue. The percentage of revenue that I deem acceptable will vary by industry, but for outsized growth prospects, I want FCF to represent at least 15% of revenue. Few companies can generate that much FCF consistently, so this requirement eliminates all but those companies with the best prospects.

Second, I look for companies that allocate capital in such a way that it generates a high FCF return on investment. Stated differently, I want companies that invest to generate even more FCF to retain flexibility in their capital structure. As long as the FCF as a percentage of revenue is sustained above 10% consistently, it means that management is allocating capital efficiently and creating a decent FCF return on invested capital.

However, not all industries can generate strong FCF, so to justify purchasing companies that do not meet the high standard mentioned above, I require companies to generate FCF as a percentage of revenue that is equal to or greater than the industry average. Industries such as utilities are heavily dependent upon debt to maintain operations and generate very little FCF, but these companies are regulated by state and local governments. This allows utilities and other companies in regulated industries to price products and services at levels that generate a reasonable rate of return on capital and the ability to pay shareholders a higher-than-market average dividend yield.

Other industries are also capital-intensive but destined to grow due to population growth or other macroeconomic forces. If the yield and dividend growth potential are sustainable in the long term, such companies can provide a solid foundation for moderate but sustainable growth for a well-diversified portfolio.

Diversification

I know I have mentioned this before, but I decided to reiterate it because it is important to keep your risk levels at tolerable levels. The importance of diversification should not be underestimated. If you hold more than 5% of your portfolio in one stock, you are probably accepting too much risk. We all make mistakes in investing over our lifetimes, so diversification helps to lessen the sting of any one investment when it goes awry.

If you own stocks in 40 companies, for example, averaging 2.5% of your portfolio in each company, when one company goes bankrupt, you can only lose 2.5% of your portfolio. If you hold 10% of your portfolio in one company that goes bankrupt, your portfolio will lose 10% of its value.

Another way to look at diversification is to consider holding different classes of assets, such as stocks, bonds, and real estate. In a bad recession, the Fed will always lower interest rates to jump-start the economy. When interest rates go down, bond prices rise leading to appreciation on the bond portion of your portfolio. Stock prices go down at the beginning of a recession, so the loss on stock can be offset by gains in bonds. Real estate can go its own way, and price movements are usually more regional, so the correlation with stocks and bonds is lower, meaning that your real estate portion of a portfolio can move independently from either stock or bond holdings.

The whole point of diversification is to not put too much of your money into one investment so that you do not risk losing too much from one bad investment decision. If you stick with quality, you are less likely to lose, and your portfolio is more likely to bounce back from any setbacks more quickly than if you hold assets of lower quality.

Finally, we need to remember that we are not investing to achieve a dollar amount goal at some point in the future. Rather, we are aiming to achieve a sustainable income goal in the future. To do that, we need to keep adding layers of income, each of which will grow year after year, one upon the other, until our future income needs are met. And since we focus most of our investments on stocks with rising dividends or rental real estate with rising rental income, we can reasonably expect to stay ahead of inflation over time. Inflation will probably average 2.5% to 3% over the long term, so if our dividend and rental income increase annually by an average of 4% or more in aggregate, our income will rise faster than inflation. That means that we should never need to sell assets to meet our budget needs.

There is a strategy called the 4% rule. It means that, in retirement, investors can withdraw 4% of their portfolio value each year and expect the portfolio to last indefinitely. But if those investors are invested primarily in stocks that do not pay dividends, they are leaving themselves in a precarious position. What happens when the stock market drops by 30-50%?

Two things: First, their annual withdrawal will drop by about the same amount, and second, they will need their portfolio holdings to increase by 43% - 100% just to get back to where they were before the market drop. Growth stocks that do not pay dividends are fine when we are younger but create too much risk for later in life. Putting yourself in such a precarious position, especially after the age of 60, can cause you to make irrational decisions in the heat of the moment. Too much risk in a portfolio at any age often leads to bad decisions when volatility kicks up. Investing for future income lets me sleep better knowing I am still on the right path to reach my goals no matter what happens to the overall market from one year to the next.

Chapter 27:
Stick to the Plan! Deviate
at Your Own Risk

Temporary vs Prolonged Deviations

Short, temporary deviations from the plan are normal. A market correction (10% drop) or even a bear market (stocks down 20% or more) are normal occurrences for which we cannot plan. But, over the long term, the stock market will recover and move higher than before. It always has and always will, but at times, it will not seem like it. At those times, when it feels like everything is falling apart and the market is down by 30% or more, it is really time to hunt for bargains.

Do you go shopping for new towels and linens right after a retailer announces a big price increase? Of course not! You go buy new stuff when your old stuff is getting worn, and you notice a big sale: 50% off! Right? Investing in stocks of great companies is no different. Pile up cash from dividends and savings and buy during a big sale.

You do not need to wait for a market crash to buy, though. Just until a great company goes on sale, it happens to a few every few years. I will give you an example:

Nvidia (ticker: NVDA) is at the bleeding edge of AI (Artificial Intelligence). The company was my first-ever recommendation back in 2000 when it was trading around $15. The stock has split four times since then, so an initial position of 100 shares (bought in 2000 for $1,500) would now be 6000 shares, and the split-adjusted entry price would be under $0.25. The stock rose to over $30 during 2001 but fell hard during the Dot Com crash that followed and was back under $5 by 2002. That was when the company was just the leading producer of graphics chips. Now, Nvidia stock trades at about $121 per share. A $1500 investment in 2000 would now be worth over $725,000. Nvidia needs to be in the growth portion of my portfolio because its dividend yield is minuscule. It is just one of the most incredible stories that most investors are aware of that makes my point.

Even when the company went down along with most technology stocks in 2022, it fell from a high of $330 in the fall of 2021 to a low of $108 the next year. That was another buying opportunity. Today (June 10, 2024), it trades at over $121 (this is on the first trading day after the company split its stock 10 for 1). It clocks in with a gain of over 340% over the last year. The point is that you do not need to be right on every stock pick to do well. You just need one or two good ones and a few more above-average picks to reach your goals over a lifetime. Gains of this nature in the growth portion of my portfolio require me to take at least partial profits and reinvest the proceeds into income-producing alternatives.

Another form of temporary deviation is when you stop saving temporarily to buy something you need, like a new car, or to pay for some emergency repairs to your house. But once that is taken care of, you get back to your plan. The point is that temporary deviations last a few months or maybe a year. A longer deviation creates a setback that is hard to come back from. Extended deviations will find you needing to plan for a later retirement.

A prolonged deviation is when you stop saving or draw money out and remain on the sidelines for several years, putting a big hole in your progress. This is especially problematic if you do it early in life. It becomes less of a big deal once you have reached the $300,000 savings threshold. That is when most people will experience their portfolio growing by more, on average, each year than they usually add through saving.

Living a little better can come after you have built a good foundation. Otherwise, as stated before, you will need to plan to work longer and retire later.

Good vs. Bad Deviations

If you decide to buy a house during a buyers' market in real estate, it should be a good long-term investment decision. It can lock in your shelter expenses with a fixed-rate mortgage instead of paying increased rent every year. But do not forget that there will be maintenance and repair expenses.

That means you need to make sure that there are no hidden costs embedded in the property you want to purchase. Make sure you make the purchase agreement contingent upon a home inspection; it could save you thousands of dollars or help you realize that the house you are considering is not the great deal you originally thought.

Buying a house sight unseen is usually an unwise decision. You always need to know what you are buying before you sign anything. Buying a house at the top of the market will lead to a lot of consternation in the years that follow until the market rebounds again. Being underwater (a mortgage balance is more than the value of your home) can lead to additional bad decisions. Avoid overpaying for a home, and always plan on living in your home for at least five years after you move in. It can often take that long before you can sell your home for an amount that leaves you with enough built-up equity for another down payment on your next home due to closing costs and repairs to generate the optimal selling price.

Buying a new car every two to three years is a waste of money. It may make you feel good at the moment, but when you check your progress toward your financial goals, it will show up as a habit that acts like an anchor that keeps dragging you from meeting your milestones as planned. Conversely, buying a new car whenever the average monthly cost of maintaining the old one starts to be more than the monthly payment on a new one makes sense. But pulling money out of your retirement savings is not the best solution.

There are any number of scenarios and spending habits that I will not bother to list as it could fill an entire book and there are already plenty of such books available. Just try to make good choices that allow you to keep putting money into your savings.

Starting Late vs Early

The first years are always the hardest, no matter when you start. The earlier you start, the better. It may not seem like you can make much progress when you are in your twenties or early thirties, but it does make hitting later milestones much easier once you build the foundation. Go back to the chart that shows how long it takes the average person to save their first $100,000. Once you get there, it gets a little easier.

Each milestone after that is a little less daunting, and when you reach that magic number of $300,000, it becomes second nature with your money working for you and doing much of the heavy lifting, as long as you keep saving and do not make withdrawals.

But if you wait until you are 40 years old or later, as most people do, you will have a much more challenging time making the progress you need to reach your retirement goals. Remember, time is a big part of what makes your plan work. It is even more important than the selection process. You can make a lot of mistakes buying the wrong stocks along the way, but you only need a handful of great picks to do very well. If you had put $5,000 into Nvidia stock 20 years ago you could be a millionaire now just from owning that one stock. Similar success would be yours if you bought the stock of any number of great companies in the spring of 2009, after the great recession and major bottom in stocks.

Apple (ticker: AAPL) $5,000 invested in April 2009 would be worth over $212,000 now.

Microsoft (ticker: MSFT) $5,000, then would be $85,000.

Netflix (ticker: NFLX) $5,000 then would be $567,000.

Visa (ticker: V) $5,000 in April 2009 would now be $60,500.

MasterCard (ticker: MA) $5,000 in April 2009 would now be $89,850.

Amgen (ticker: AMGN) $5,000 then would be $28,000 now, plus dividends at 3%+ per year. Okay, so that is only a bit over four times your money in 14 ½ years. But that equals a compound annual growth rate of 12.6%, plus the dividends. It is hard to capture 15% annual growth in stocks consistently. Few investors, even the greatest investors, can accomplish this feat consistently over a period of more than a few years.

Of course, Amgen was the worst of all the examples listed. Imagine if you had owned two or more of these stocks over that period. Investing is not that difficult; it just takes a lot of patience to get it right.

But always remember, you are not really investing to amass a dollar amount; you are investing to build layers of future income streams that grow each year faster than inflation. All but two of these stocks also pay dividends. Apple did not at the beginning, but then instituted a dividend in 2012 and has increased that dividend handsomely every year since. The compound annual rate of dividend increase has been 8.8%. Would you like a raise of almost 9% every year, especially in retirement?

Setbacks: Unavoidable vs Self-Inflicted

I have touched on this to a certain extent above in discussing deviations. So, this will be brief and to the point.

Unavoidable setbacks come in the form of market corrections or bear markets. They can also come in the form of medical emergencies, but hopefully, you do not have cheap insurance, so most of the cost can be covered by insurance, and the rest can come from your buffer account (discussed in the next section below).

Most unavoidable setbacks will happen to everyone at the same time, but you can bounce back from these setbacks and get back on track because that is just how the market works. Your portfolio could be down by as much as 30% over a two-year period, but you will experience a strong bull market over the next several years that put you back on track with above-average gains as discussed in the section above. It only takes a few great stocks to excel at investing. That is why selectivity is important.

Plus, if you are collecting cash from dividends and savings, waiting for bargain buying opportunities, only a portion of your savings will be negatively impacted. Once the worst is over, you can enhance your rebound by taking advantage of buying stocks of great companies on sale!

One other aspect of buying high-quality, dividend-paying stocks is that they usually fall less than the overall market. That is because smart, long-term investors like us hold onto quality through all the ups and downs since we know those stocks will bounce back faster than lower-quality stocks.

Self-inflicted setbacks are hard to recover from. This is when you decide to sell some of your portfolio stocks to buy a new car or when you sell your stocks near the bottom because you got scared. This last one is the bane of most small investors. You never know when a stock market correction is going to happen, but you should always know that it will end eventually and that after that bottom, there will be great buying opportunities. Nothing lasts forever; neither the best of times nor the worst of times.

Create Buffer Savings

The best way to avoid early withdrawals or unexpected expenses is to be prepared for the unexpected.

The best way to be prepared is to set aside a small amount of savings each month in what I call a "buffer" account. You can call it whatever you want, but its purpose should remain the same: to have money to cover planned and unplanned major expenses that will arise over a lifetime.

Examples are:

Downpayment for a house.

Downpayment for a new car.

New appliances when one or more break down or remodeling a room, like a kitchen or bath.

Repairs or replacements to your home such as roof, HVAC system, water leaks: tree roots damaging sidewalks, foundation, exterior water line, etc.; natural disasters not covered by insurance; etc.

Medical emergencies.

Weddings (yours or for a daughter) can be expensive these days.

Vacations (something we all need but do not always have the money to afford what we want).

The list could go on, but I just wanted to name a few that most of us have experienced by the time we are ready to retire. In terms of the home expenses (and several of those multiple times), the cost of those experiences can run $10,000 or more per incident. Owning a home is good for containing the monthly cost of housing, but it can also be expensive on the maintenance side of the equation. The point is that most of you reading this have either experienced most of the above or know someone who has; they happen to all of us.

Interlude 6: A Personal Perspective

This one is a little close to home, so I will not be naming names. Two of my siblings became millionaires, and the other died prematurely of brain cancer. Most of my nieces and nephews have achieved financial freedom. None of them are pretentious or live ostentatiously. They all lived within their means and saved or invested in themselves (their businesses or education).

My point is that no matter what career you choose, you can find a way to accomplish your financial goals if you are willing to create a plan and stick to it.

Living comfortably in retirement is often attained by living modestly for the first couple of decades until one has accumulated enough or progressed in their career to a point when saving no longer requires sacrifice. But getting to that point may mean not buying a new car as often as one would like, not paying for cable TV, not eating out as often, or maybe finding extra income to supplement a primary job.

My wife and I sacrificed in a few of these ways, enabling me to retire at the age of 52 so I could spend more time with our children. I really enjoyed coaching soccer and building sets for the spring musical. I even enjoyed taking one to dance classes, packing lunches, and walking them to and from the bus stop when they were young. That was so much better than working ten-hour days and commuting an hour each way to and from work.

I started out delivering mail for the U.S. Postal Service. I became a staff accountant at the national headquarters after earning a CPA credential. I moved from accounting to an evaluation analyst position and eventually ended up as Manager of Corporate Alliances. I never made a six-figure salary on my own but with what my wife made, we did exceed that income level for a few years.

We lived a few blocks from a college campus, so to generate a little more income, we remodeled the basement and rented it out along with two spare bedrooms. My wife and I, plus our firstborn, slept in what was designed to be a family room with a full bathroom. I just added doors for privacy from the rest of the house. We only did that for three or four years. Then our second child came, and we decided to reclaim our home and spread out a little more comfortably. By that time, I had been promoted three times and was making almost double what I had been making when we moved to the area. My wife's income had also increased, so we were at the point where we could enjoy life a little more. But kids are expensive, so we occasionally had to rein in our spending to keep saving according to our plan.

Our net worth reached $1 million by my 51st birthday and the Postal Service was offering people in my unit an early retirement option. I will admit that there have been some years when I wondered if I had done the right thing in retiring early but, looking back, I have no regrets.

We may have made sacrifices that most people would not consider, but it got us to where we wanted to be when we wanted to be there.

Part VII:
Analysis and Tools I Use

Chapter 28:
Dividend-Paying Stocks

Finding Quality Dividend-Paying Companies

A good place to start is with a list of stocks that consistently raise dividends every year. I like those with a history of doing so for at least 10 years. Most of these companies were able to raise dividends even during the Financial Crisis, and the list is called the Dividend Achievers. The list is updated annually, and you can search for it by year (best to use the current year list because companies can drop off the list for cutting the dividend, and only those that continue to raise stay on it; also, it includes the most recent additions).

You will notice that there are other lists linked to that site. Dividend Aristocrats and Champions are those companies with a minimum of at least 25 years of annual dividend increases. The difference between the two is simply that Aristocrats are also components of the S&P 500, while Champions are not limited to the index. Again, you can find these lists by searching for Dividend Aristocrats or Dividend Champions.

Dividend Kings, of which there are fewer, have raised their dividends for at least 50 years consecutively.

That gives you a starting place. Drilling down to find the best quality among those companies gets harder. I use the Friedrich algorithm as a shortcut to help me with that. If you prefer to do it all by hand, I'll list my checklist, but the algorithm saves me time that I would rather spend on other things. It is not free (cost is $1,000 per year or $250 per quarter, making it more affordable for those who only want to check in a few times a year), but it does the heavy lifting analysis. I still dig into companies more for my own peace of mind, but I do not have to dig as much or as often.

Full Disclosure: I also want you to be aware that I have partnered with the creator of Friedrich and now offer it as a tool through the Seeking Alpha Marketplace. So, I am biased but would not use or promote something unless I trusted it.

My Quality Checklist

First, I look for consistency over at least five years of results. I do not require a company to be superior to its competitors in every category every year, but I do like it to be at least equal to or above the average for its industry for every category. Here is my list (in no specific order):

- Dividend yield of 2% or more.

- Dividend Payout ratio that is equal to or less than the industry average.

- Dividend growth of at least 6% per year over the last ten years.

(Note: I will sometimes consider a company that pays either a higher dividend with slower growth or one that has a lower dividend with a much higher rate of growth – I am more interested in what the yield will likely be in 30 years than what it is today; meaning that the 2% yield is a rule of thumb). □

- Debt to Total Assets that is equal to or lower than the industry average.

- Goodwill that is equal to less than 50% of total assets.

- Consistent GAAP earnings and revenue growth over at least the last five year that is equal to or above the industry average.

- Consistently superior FCF (Free Cash Flow) compared to the industry average over at least the last five years.

- Operating margins that are consistently equal to or higher than the industry average.

- ROIC (Return on Invested Capital) that is consistently equal to or higher than the industry average.

- The best value that is based upon the Price to FCF ratio.

Stock Rover

To find industry averages and at least 10 years of data for each company there are several options. My preference is Stock Rover because it calculates all the ratios I need and provides industry averages that I can compare to all for a lower fee than most other sources I have tried.

Fridrich Global Research

I have an association with Friedrich Global Research and earn a portion of any revenue that comes in through my efforts. The price of the service is the same whether you go directly to the company or through my website.

The advantage of the Friedrich algorithm is that it provides a database of analysis on over 20,000 stocks from 36 countries around the world, with 10 years of ratios on U.S. stocks and 5 years of ratios on foreign stocks. It is all color-coded to make it easy to determine quality and consistency. Below is an example of a Friedrich data file and one of a Friedrich chart:

Apple Inc	October 26, 2023	MARGIN OF SAFETY	16%	FRIEDRICH FINAL FOUR	0	SUPER SIX SCORE	4	TTM DATA DATE	June 30, 2023	Apple Inc	TYPE OF ANALYSIS
WWW.ASKFRIEDRICH.CO	2014	2015	2016	2017	2018	2019	2020	2021	2022	TTM	WWW.ASKFRIEDRICH.CO	CEI ADVISORS
Wall Street Price	$24.91	$27.70	$28.13	$38.45	$56.82	$55.99	$116.50	$139.14	$142.45	$167.54	Wall Street Price	Quantitative
Main Street Price	$33.37	$55.04	$35.33	$41.90	$67.22	$68.64	$89.16	$212.73	$240.39	$199.27	Main Street Price	Quantitative
Bargain Price	$22.25	$39.36	$23.55	$27.93	$44.82	$45.76	$59.44	$141.82	$160.26	$132.85	Bargain Price	Quantitative
Sell Price	$55.63	$98.43	$58.89	$69.85	$112.06	$114.42	$148.63	$354.63	$400.73	$132.18	Sell Price	Quantitative
SUPER SIX SCORE	5	6	3	5	5	4	5	6	6	4	SUPER SIX SCORE	Qualitative
Bargain Price	$22.25	$39.36	$23.55	$27.93	$44.82	$45.76	$59.44	$160.26	$160.26	$132.85	Bargain Price	Quantitative
FROIC Ratio	29%	41%	19%	22%	34%	31%	48%	75%	73%	50%	FROIC Ratio	Qualitative
CAPFLOW Ratio	20%	17%	23%	21%	19%	15%	11%	10%	10%	11%	CAPFLOW Ratio	Qualitative
Badwill To Price Ratio	1%	1%	1%	0%	0%	0%	0%	0%	0%	0%	Badwill To Price Ratio	Qualitative
Friedrich Cash Machine	22.9%	25.8%	21.9%	21.7%	24.0%	24.8%	25.6%	32.1%	32.7%	30.8%	Friedrich Cash Machine	Qualitative
Friedrich Equalizer	29.8%	53.7%	14.2%	28.0%	39.8%	22.7%	31.1%	65.3%	40.5%	28.2%	Friedrich Equalizer	Quantitative
Super Three Criteria											Super Three Criteria	
Friedrich R Ratio	85%	100%	65%	89%	85%	75%	65%	90%	90%	50%	Friedrich R Ratio	Qualitative
Relative Risk Ratio	0%	0%	0%	0%	0%	0%	0%	0%	0%	0%	Relative Risk Ratio	Qualitative
Revenue Growth Ratio	7%	28%	8%	6%	16%	2%	6%	33%	8%	3%	Revenue Growth Ratio	Quantitative
Michaelis Ratio	27%	37%	28%	28%	44%	47%	67%	125%	160%	133%	Michaelis Ratio	Qualitative
Watson Ratio	97%	105%	93%	97%	99%	103%	107%	103%	101%	99%	Watson Ratio	Qualitative
Mycroft Yield Ratio	7%	10%	8%	6%	6%	7%	4%	6%	6%	5%	Mycroft Yield Ratio	Quantitative
Psaras Ratio	42%	22%	44%	42%	32%	33%	39%	13%	12%	19%	Psaras Ratio	Quantitative
Mycroft Michaelis Growth	21%	26%	17%	16%	23%	25%	29%	47%	58%	51%	Mycroft Michaelis Growth	Qualitative
Mycroft PEG Ratio	47%	25%	68%	76%	51%	49%	67%	23%	21%	34%	Mycroft PEG Ratio	Qualitative
Synthesis Ratio	5	5	3	0	4	4	4	5	5	3	Synthesis Ratio	Qualitative
Creative Criteria	1	4	1	0	0	0	0	1	1	0	Creative Criteria	Qualitative
Altman Z Non-Financials	5.15	4.37	3.76	3.66	4.37	4.35	6.51	7.04	6.80	8.11	Altman Z Non-Financials	Quantitative
Altman Z Financials Score	8.25	6.87	6.22	6.04	6.92	7.33	10.67	10.93	10.03	12.49	Altman Z Financials Score	Quantitative
Piotroski F Score	N/A	N/A	5	4	6	7	7	7	7	6	Piotroski F Score	Quantitative
Fraud Center											Fraud Center	
Beneish Score	N/A	-2.88	-2.92	-2.73	-2.68	-3.11	-3.02	-2.65	-2.82	-3.21	Beneish Score	Quantitative
Badwill To Price Ratio	1%	1%	1%	0%	0%	0%	0%	0%	0%	0%	Badwill To Price Ratio	Quantitative
Sherlock Debt Divisor	$25.08	$29.62	$30.25	$41.76	$60.73	$57.86	$119.94	$165.05	$145.65	$173.84	Sherlock Debt Divisor	Quantitative
Buffett Grade Ratio	90%	100%	60%	80%	90%	70%	90%	90%	90%	90%	Buffett Grade Ratio	Quantitative
Mycroft FCF Per Share	$1.87	$2.90	$2.31	$2.54	$3.51	$3.85	$4.51	$8.29	$9.68	$8.92	Mycroft FCF Per Share	Quantitative
Price to Mycroft FCF	13.85	10.21	13.09	16.44	17.33	15.02	26.57	17.51	15.47	19.48	Price to Mycroft FCF	Quantitative
Bernhard/Buffet FCF	$1.55	$2.30	$1.98	$2.19	$2.86	$3.08	$3.49	$5.63	$6.14	$5.92	Bernhard/Buffet FCF	Quantitative
Price to Bernhard/Buffet	16.73	12.85	15.34	19.04	21.26	18.77	34.38	25.78	24.38	29.36	Price to Bernhard/Buffet	Quantitative
Lori Turbo Ratio	0.32	0.60	0.34	0.35	0.65	0.77	1.02	2.66	3.54	5.08	Lori Turbo Ratio	Qualitative
Right Time Ratio	0.53	0.23	0.89	0.87	0.52	0.63	0.45	0.25	0.31	0.52	Right Time Ratio	Quantitative
Sherlock PE Ratio	35.08	10.45	15.81	17.07	17.61	19.88	34.73	19.39	22.71	30.04	Sherlock PE Ratio	Quantitative
Sherlock Price to Book	568%	575%	520%	654%	1134%	1181%	3218%	3878%	4824%	4558%	Sherlock Price to Book	Quantitative
Munger Ratio	0.51	0.24	0.82	0.79	0.52	0.65	0.88	0.26	0.31	0.52	Munger Ratio	Qualitative
Mario Ratio	1.90	4.30	1.13	1.22	1.91	1.59	1.22	4.02	3.24	1.91	Mario Ratio	Qualitative
Williams Ratio	100%	100%	0%	100%	100%	0%	0%	100%	100%	0%	Williams Ratio	Qualitative
Badwill Ratio	$0.36	$0.39	$0.39	$0.00	$0.00	$0.00	$0.00	$0.00	$0.00	$0.00	Badwill Ratio	Qualitative
Final Test Score	80%	90%	70%	80%	80%	80%	80%	80%	90%	70%	Final Test Score	Quantitative
Bankers Loan Ratio	3.95	2.82	2.64	3.15	2.97	3.03	3.19	2.34	2.27	2.17	Bankers Loan Ratio	Quantitative

You can find explanations of each ratio displayed on our website: AskFriedrich.com.

	2014	2015	2016	2017	2018	2019	2020	2021	2022	TTM
SUPER SIX SCORE	5	6	3	5	5	4	5	6	6	4
WALL STREET PRICE	$24.91	$27.70	$28.13	$38.45	$56.82	$55.99	$116.50	$139.14	$142.45	$167.54
MAIN STREET PRICE	$33.37	$59.04	$35.33	$41.90	$67.22	$68.64	$89.16	$212.73	$240.39	$199.27
OVERBOUGHT	$55.63	$98.43	$58.89	$69.85	$112.06	$114.42	$148.63	$354.63	$400.73	$332.18
OVERSOLD	$22.25	$39.36	$23.55	$27.93	$44.82	$45.76	$59.44	$141.82	$160.26	$132.85

WWW.ASKFRIEDRICH.COM

The chart is easier to understand. The white line is the Wall Street Price (market price); the yellow line is the Main Street Price (algorithm's fair value); the red line is the Sell Price (66% above fair value); and the green line is the algorithm's bargain price (33% below fair value). TTM stands for trailing twelve months. The TTM calculation is updated monthly. All other prices are as of calendar year end.

In this instance, the market price of Apple (AAPL) was below the fair value, indicating that Apple stock was undervalued and could be bought. Of course, the optimal time to have bought Apple stock was in 2015, when the market price fell below the bargain price. All prices are adjusted for stock splits.

I want to call your attention to the historical success rate of the algorithm now, as that is what caught my eye in the first place. The 60-year back test, which can be found on the AskFriedrich.com website and is also included as an appendix to this book, shows us two particularly important things:

- Investing in quality can provide much higher total returns over the long term than just investing in a market index. (21% vs 6.8%)

- Investing over an extended period in stocks can yield incredible returns if done right.

Appendix B provides the entire back test covering the period from January 1, 1960, through December 31, 2009. Ending in the year 2009 was on purpose since it was a year in which stocks had hit a major bottom and just begun to rebound. Therefore, it was not the optimal time to end the test period to achieve the best results.

The Friedrich method of FCF investing beat the Dow Jones Industrial Average (DJIA) in 55 of 60 years. $10,000 invested in the DJIA over the 60-year test period turned into $511,469.76. The same $10,000 invested using the Friedrich method turned into $965,001,511. So, would you rather have half a million dollars or nearly one billion? Choosing quality matters, and sticking to a proven system can make an enormous difference.

Chapter 29:
Growth Stocks

The perfect use of the Friedrich algorithm is to identify stocks with outstanding future growth potential. Wall Street would have investors jump into and out of stocks for growth. That, to me, is a fool's errand. I also believe that no more than 20% of one's portfolio should be committed specifically to growth without concern for dividend income. The creator of Friedrich would disagree with me on this point. No matter. The algorithm can be used to identify growth stocks with low-risk profiles and consistently superior dividend-paying stocks.

The younger an investor is, the more s/he can focus on growth if they want. But never lose sight of the end goal of creating enough income to retire comfortably. The example of Apple stock that I used earlier could have been a dividend stock when first purchased since it had a yield above 2% with excellent growth prospects for the future. Now, it would need to be held as part of the growth portion of a portfolio, even though it does pay a dividend because the yield has fallen due to the price rising faster than the dividend increases. However, the dividend keeps rising at an above-average rate, thus making the future income stream another important aspect of the holding.

I am not recommending that people go out and buy Apple stock! The earlier example is merely an example from one point in time. It may be months or even years later that you are reading this book since I initially wrote this section.

Growth stocks will tend to rise more rapidly in good years and fall much faster and further in bad years than quality dividend-paying stocks. The purpose of having a portion of your portfolio devoted to growth is not so much to accumulate wealth (because it can disappear as fast as it was created) but to generate value that can be realized (through the sale of stocks that become overpriced) that can then be invested in dividend-paying stocks when bargains arise.

I prefer to only buy growth stocks in a tax-deferred account, so I do not have to pay taxes on my gains. This is critical to holding onto as much of your hard-earned gains as possible until you reach retirement. I have no problem with taking gains on a stock that has become overvalued when it is held in a tax-deferred account.

In my accounts that are not tax-deferred, I stick with those stocks that I plan to hold forever for the income they provide me, now and in the future.

The problem that I have with buying and holding small capitalization growth stocks is that growth tends to happen without the foundation of fundamental operating results, such as the generation of free cash flow (or sometimes without earnings). Revenue growth is fine if operating margins are improving consistently and moving toward profitability and free cash flow generation. The other problem is that growth stocks tend to be far more volatile than dividend-paying stocks. Maybe I just do not like riding the roller coaster market, and I like to sleep at night, but dividends give me peace of mind and are the building blocks for a comfortable retirement.

More about the Back Test

I want to use the following table taken from the back test to make a few points. First, when you invest in quality companies, you experience higher returns more often and fewer negative return years than when investing in an index. A few examples to look at below: 1957, 1962, 1963, 1965, 1966, 1969, 1973, 1974, 1977, 1978, 1981, 1984, 2000, 2001, 2002, 2005, and 2008. In each of those years, DJIA was negative. Also, in those same years, stocks chosen using the Price to Free Cash Flow (FCF) method returns were either positive (11 instances) or generated smaller losses (6 instances). The Price to FCF selections beat DJIA in 55 out of 60 years. Nothing is perfect, but this is about as close as it gets. Avoiding big losses is a particularly important key to successful investing.

The other thing I want you to notice is that not only did the Price to FCF method consistently beat DJIA returns year after year, but there are many instances where it did so by exceptionally large margins. Examples where the Price to FCF method more than doubled the DJIA returns (not including those 11 instances where the Price to FCF method returns were positive and DJIA was negative): 1952, 1956, 1967, 1970, 1976, 1979, 1980, 1982, 1987, 1991, 1992, 1993, 1994, 1998, 2004, and 2007. All totaled, there were 16 years where the returns were doubled using the Price to FCF method and 11 more where the returns were positive while DJIA was negative. So, in 27 of 60 years, this method created returns that more than doubled those of DJIA. That is how growth investing is supposed to work!

Year	Price to Free Cash Flow	DJIA
1950	+31.13%	+17.62%
1951	+28.05%	+14.36%
1952	+16.88%	+0.51%
1953	+4.77%	+3.80%
1954	+64.80%	+43.96%
1955	+29.42%	+20.77%
1956	+13.86%	+2.27%
1957	+11.52%	-12.77%
1958	+52.66%	+33.96%
1959	+26.94%	+16.39%
1960	-15.20%	-9.34%
1961	+33.23%	+18.72%
1962	+12.12%	-10.81%
1963	+43.86%	-17.00%
1964	+18.81%	+14.57%
1965	+22.34%	-10.88%
1966	-9.40%	-18.94%
1967	+34.65%	+15.20%
1968	+6.99%	+4.26%

Year	Price to Free Cash Flow	DJIA
1969	-0.33%	-15.19%
1970	+31.82%	+4.82%
1971	+1.57%	+6.11%
1972	+27.32%	+14.58%
1973	+14.54%	-19.38%
1974	+19.51%	-25.05%
1975	+52.85%	+38.32%

1976	+46.48%	+17.86%
1977	-1.77%	-17.26%
1978	+12.45%	-3.15%
1979	+18.57%	+4.19%
1980	+33.57%	+14.93%
1981	+10.62%	-9.23%
1982	+55.82%	+19.60%
1983	+35.23%	+20.26%
1984	+6.49%	-3.73%
1985	+35.77%	+27.66%
1986	+35.17%	+22.58%
1987	+34.19%	+2.26%
1988	+23.44%	+11.85%
1989	+35.96%	+26.96%
1990	-27.16%	-4.36%
1991	+99.09%	+20.32%
1992	+23.17%	+4.17%
1993	+34.21%	+13.72%
1994	+14.20%	+2.14%
1995	+32.84%	+33.45%
1996	+21.72%	+26.01%
1997	+36.30%	+22.64%
1998	+37.71%	+16.10%
1999	+16.50%	+25.22%
2000	+19.96%	-6.17%
2001	-3.91%	-7.10%
2002	-3.58%	-15.87%

2003	+28.96%	+23.98%
2004	+8.94%	+3.14%
2005	+3.41%	-0.11%
2006	+31.10%	+16.29%
2007	+16.72%	+6.37%
2008	-22.39%	-32.71%
2009	+22.95%	+15.43%

But an investor need not be right on every investment decision s/he makes. It only takes one or two highly successful positions in each year to beat the market indices. I will not recreate more of the back test here, but I would like to draw your attention to Part 3, where it shows the individual purchases in each year of the full period.

In the first year, there were four outstanding picks that generated returns of more than 50% each, two of which were over 70%. You also do not need to have a great year every year since some years can provide a significant boost to overall returns. For example, in 1954, ten of 13 picks achieved returns over 50%, with two over 100%. The full return for that year was 64.80%. Over the full 60 years there were just four years that the Price to FCF selections were over 50%, with 1991 achieving a return of 99.09% (as you can see in the table above). In that year there were only three stocks that met the requirements with returns of 36.61%, 57.90%, and 202.76%. With one-third of a portfolio returning over 200% for the year, the overall return became extraordinary. Of course, if the growth portion of your portfolio is limited to 20% or less, the boost to your overall portfolio will be less, but it can help you achieve above-average overall returns just the same. Committing more than 20% can lead to unnecessary levels of risk.

To put things into perspective, as I write this paragraph on December 30, 2023, one of the stocks that met our criteria at the beginning of the year was Lam Research (LRCX), which gained 87.74% for the year. Another, Netflix (NFLX), achieved a return of 68.49%. Another, Apple (AAPL), gained 49.36% that year. Finally, Meta (META), another that met our requirements, gained 197.95% for 2023. The point I am trying to make here is that the methodology still works. It is not just something that worked way back when. The Friedrich Algorithm is alive and well.

The other point is that sticking with quality helps to insulate a portfolio during the worst years for market returns. Notice in the table above that in 2000, the Price to FCF portfolio returned +19.96% while DJIA registered a loss of -6.17%. It was because one of the companies selected for our portfolio gained over 100% during the early part of the recession. Quality matters!

And finding quality companies at bargain prices is what Friedrich does very consistently. You can learn more about the Friedrich system at askfriedrich.com. Access to the explanation of all the ratios used by the algorithm is free, but a subscription to the monthly analysis of all stocks is not. It only makes sense to subscribe annually if one already has at least $100,000 in a stock portfolio. Another option for smaller portfolio investors is to use the quarterly subscription periodically (once or twice a year) when reviewing one's holdings.

Options

I do not recommend the use of options for beginners, but for those who have been investing for five or more years, there are a few strategies that can help boost your income and/or growth in any given year if applied properly and in the appropriate economic/market environment.

One such strategy is called Optionistics and was developed by a friend of mine. He was able to turn about $214,000 into $1,370,000 over ten years. The account still has $762,000 in it after he periodically withdrew $608,000, which dramatically undermined the results he would have achieved had he kept that money working in the system as well. He made a lot of mistakes along the way but has recently made several improvements that will protect his holding from significant losses. Once it is tested further and ready to launch, I will provide more information on my website at BernFactor.com (after I test it myself, of course).

Other Last-Minute Tidbits

Once this book has been published, I plan to launch a subscription-based newsletter on SeekingAlpha.com (a free website) to provide investors with a real-time inside look at how I manage my own portfolio, including announcements of purchases and sales of individual stocks, bonds, and options, along with explanations of why each investment appeals to me at the time of purchase or no longer fits my portfolio requirements.

I will also include links on BernFactor.com to helpful sources of information and stock tools that I use for data analysis, as well as links to some of my recently published articles available to the public. I plan to develop some helpful downloadable applications that can be used by beginners and experienced investors alike to create goals, track progress, analyze a portfolio, and create links. My plan is to keep the annual fees low so more people can afford to benefit from them, not just the wealthy.

Chapter 30:
Setting Goals

The first application is in the works and should be available by the time this book is published (or soon after – check the BernFactor website). It is designed to be customized for any investor with any level of income. The first tab will include inputs that can be entered at the beginning of the journey and modified at any time along the way, even years into the future, as circumstances change. It will look something like this below. All the inputs will be blank when downloaded but I decided to enter inputs to provide a sense of what it would look like when filled out.

Inputs and Assumptions
When you see a (:), please enter

Input in the column next to it.

Date of Birth: 6/8/2000

Today's Date: 12/31/2023

Age: 24

Year Started: 3

Current Income: 20000

Est. Ave. Income Growth: 4%

Est. Ave. L/T Inflation Rate: 3%

Est. Annual Dividend Growth: 6%

401K Inputs

Initial Annual % Contribution: 3%

Est. Ave. Fund Growth/Year: 7%

Year of 1st % Contr. Increase: 2

Year of 2nd % Contr. Increase: 5

Year of 3rd % Contr. Increase: 10

Year of 4th % Contr. Increase: 12
Year of 4th % Contr. Increase: 18

Year of 5th % Contr. Increase: 19

Year of 6th % Contr. Increase: 19

Year of 7th % Contr. Increase: 22

Year of 8th % Contr. Increase: 23

Company % Match Contr.: 3%

IRA Assumptions

Year Started: 5

Est. Ave. Fund Growth/Year: 8%

Initial Contribution: $2,500

Contribution Increase: 500

Year of 1st Contr. Increase: 8

Year of 2nd Contr. Increase: 12

Year of 3rd Contr. Increase: 15

Year of 4th Contr. Increase: 18

Year of 5th Contr. Increase: 21

Year of 6th Contr. Increase: 24

Year of 7th Contr. Increase: 27

Year of 8th Contr. Increase: 30

Year of 9th Contr. Increase: 32
Taxable Assumptions:

Year Started: 10

Est. Ave. Fund Growth/Year: 8%

Initial Contribution: 3000

Contribution Increase: 1000

Year of 1st % Contr. Increase: 12

Year of 2nd Contr. Increase: 14

Year of 3rd Contr. Increase: 15

Year of 4th Contr. Increase: 18

Year of 5th Contr. Increase: 20

Year of 6th Contr. Increase: 22

Year of 7th Contr. Increase: 25

There will be individual tabs for each type of savings account an investor has, including 401K, IRA, Taxable brokerage accounts, and Drip Investments (another form of taxable account). Each will show year-by-year estimates and cumulative totals. There will also be a page that estimates total savings and another that projects total income from all investment accounts by year so you can keep tabs on your progress from either angle.

The application will allow people to use their own estimate of what they expect inflation to be over the long term and will then extrapolate how much income they will need to live comfortably in the future based upon what they need in the present. It also estimates social security income based upon the average annual amount received by current retirees. That, of course, will vary greatly depending on each individual's income and depending on what changes Congress inflicts upon us in the future.

We will also design it for up to two users, showing estimated results for each user separately, as well as combined total pages for total assets and future income.

We also plan to create a feedback loop so users can tell us how we might make it more useful in future iterations.

Appendix C includes a few screenshots of what it would look like with the inputs shown above.

Appendix A
Guiding Principles

1. You are investing for future income, layering new streams of income, one upon another, that will grow over time, doubling repeatedly. You are not to worry about how much your portfolio is worth because that is not the goal. The goal is to have built up enough income to provide you with a comfortable retirement and keep you ahead of inflation so you never run out of money. Too many people focus on a total dollar value portfolio goal to attain for retirement. That effort is misguided and will, often as not, lead to an investor outliving their retirement nest egg. If your income at retirement more than meets your needs and rises faster than inflation, what does the total value of your portfolio matter? The balance will go up and down over a lifetime, but as the income keeps rising each year like clockwork, you will meet your goal if you stay the course.

2. Bonds are not always a bad investment. When interest rates are high, it is good to lock in a reliable source of steady income for a given time. The interest can be reinvested as received to achieve a rising income, as each new bond will add a new layer of interest income. As interest rates fall, the principal value of a bond rises, so there is an appreciation to be gained from buying bonds at the right time. The opposite is true in that as interest rates rise, the principal value of a bond will fall. So, when interest rates are low, bonds are rarely a safe place to invest unless the investor intends to hold the bonds until maturity for income. If the bonds are bought at face value, there will never be a loss realized unless the owner sells them before maturity. The best way to play bonds is to buy when interest rates are high and more likely to fall than rise further and to sell when interest rates are low and more likely to rise than fall further.

3. An interesting way to use bonds is to build a bond ladder with cash when stocks do not offer any good opportunities. A bond ladder consists of equally divided portions of a bond portfolio invested, each in a different maturity, preferably in one-year increments. This way, the investor will have a portion of his/her bond portfolio maturing each year, giving them the flexibility to either roll the position over into another bond position of one year longer duration than the longest maturity currently held or to invest the maturing funds into a stock that has hit their target price/value. An example would be to use one-fifth of the bond portfolio to buy one-year treasury bills, another-fifth to buy two-year treasury bills, and so on, with the last portion being invested in five-year notes.

The point of this exercise is to create income from cash that is being held while waiting for a good buying opportunity in dividend-paying stocks. Shorter maturity fixed income securities will depreciate less when interest rates fall than will longer maturity bonds. If the stock market crashes at any time while the investor is holding those fixed-income securities (assuming the investor uses Treasury securities), the flight to safety into Treasuries is more than likely to help increase the value of those securities until the Federal Reserve decides to begin cutting interest rates. So, selling those securities at the beginning of a recession will usually provide more cash for reinvestment. Then is when it requires patience as an investor.

Alternatively, the investor could just allow the fixed-income securities to mature each year and reinvest the proceeds as they become available.

4. The hardest parts of this investing strategy are getting started as early as possible, consistently adding to your portfolio, and having the patience to wait for good bargains to show themselves.

As Warren Buffett has said, "Be fearful when others are greedy, and be greedy when others are fearful." That is always harder than it sounds, but it may be the best advice he ever gave.

5. You do not need a six-figure income to become rich in the end. Achieving financial security is different for each person or family, depending on how they grew up. Teachers, secretaries, janitors, mechanics, bookkeepers, retail store workers, almost anybody can do it if they can force themselves to live within their means and put a little aside for retirement consistently over a lifetime. The best time to start is now, regardless of your current age! The sooner you start, the sooner you will begin to see the results of your efforts, and the sooner you will be able to retire. Put another way, the longer you put off starting, the longer you will need to work to meet your retirement income goals.

6. Keep your analysis simple so you can perform adequate due diligence. Keep it to a process of elimination with a maximum of 10 conditions to be met. Here are my 10: dividend yield, minimum of 10 years of increasing dividends, consistently rising revenue and earnings, goodwill that is equal to less than 50% of total assets, equal to or better than the industry average in debt level, free cash flow generation, operating margin, ROIC, payout ratio; and the best value based upon Price to FCF ratio. This checklist will help you identify quality companies with a consistently strong track record at a good price. Remember: do not be fooled by one year of good results; always look for consistency of superior results relative to peers over at least three years, preferably five years or longer. Companies that outperform their peers over long periods of time usually do so due to their ability to maintain a winning culture and business model that works through good times and bad.

Appendix B
Back Test – The Power of Free Cash Flow

It is with express permission from the author of the following published research, Mycroft Psaras and Mycroft Research, that I am allowed to present the back test results. My thanks to the author for his contribution to my book and for the tireless effort in reconstructing the results that follow.

Back test showing the power of Price to Free Cash Flow in the Investment Process

1950-2009

Mycroft Psaras

Mycroft Research, LLC

The following is a back-test that will be used as proof of just how well the component of free cash flow works in the investment process. The key formula to be used in this back-test is the one for "Price to Free Cash Flow per share," which we calculate as follows:

P/FCF = (Market Price per share)/ ((cash flow – capital spending)/ (diluted shares outstanding))).

I believe this to be the most important ratio in finance and the core foundation of all my work.

In order to validate my theories, I needed to see how a back-test of price to free cash flow per share would turn out if it were back-tested over a multi-year time from. Accordingly, I undertook a back test for the years 1950 to 2009 and used the thirty stocks that make up the Dow Jones Industrial Average (DJIA) to do so.

Starting on January 1st of each year from 1950 to 2009 inclusive, I determined which companies in the DJIA would have been purchased using companies that came in at around 15 times their price to free cash flow per share. I then purchased these companies and held them for exactly one year, selling them on December 31st of the same year. I repeated this process for all subsequent years, for a total of sixty years. The results confirm the validity of our methods and show conclusively that a free cash flow-based strategy not only works but works very well.

Specifically, in terms of relative performance, my free cash flow picks beat the DJIA in fifty-five of sixty years tested. Moreover, the average gain for the FGCF Portfolio was 21.08% per year over sixty years, compared to an average gain for the DJIA Portfolio of just 6.77% over the same sixty years. Thus, if I started with $10,000 in each of the two portfolios (FCF vs. DJIA) at the conclusion of sixty years, the DJIA would be worth $511,469.76, and the FCF portfolio would be worth $965,001,511. This means that the FCF system beat the DJIA by 1887 times, or in relative performance terms, by 188,700%.

In introducing the actual data, I have broken it down into four parts, as follows:

Part 1: The components of the DJIA for each year. Since the components were similar for many consecutive years, we decided to post the updated DJIA list only in those years where changes were made to the index.

Part 2: The side-by-side comparison of yearly percentage gain for FCF Portfolio vs that of the DJIA Index performance.

Part 3: Purchases made using "Free Cash Flow" for the years 1950-2000, which enable the performance of tach purchase to be evaluated retrospectively.

Part 4: Yearly side-by-side cumulative performance of "Free Cash Flow" vs. that of the DJIA, in actual dollars, start with $10,000 in each portfolio on January 1, 1950, and ending December 31, 2009.

Part 1

The Components of the Dow Jones Industrial Average 1950-2009

1950-1955

Allied Chemical

Allied Can

American Smelting

American Telephone & Telegraph

American Tobacco

Bethlehem Steel

Chrysler

Corn Products Refining

Du Pont

Eastman Kodak

General Electric

General Foods

General Motors

Goodyear

International Harvester

International Nickel

Johns-Manville

116

Lowe's

National Distillers

National Steel

Procter & Gamble

Sears Roebuck & Co

Standard Oil of California

Standard Oil (N.J.)

Texas Corporation

Union Carbide

United Aircraft

U.S. Steel

Westinghouse Electric

Woolworth

1956-1958

Allied Chemical

Allied Can

American Smelting

American Telephone & Telegraph

American Tobacco

Bethlehem Steel

Chrysler

Corn Products Refining

Du Pont

Eastman Kodak

General Electric

General Foods

General Motors

Goodyear

International Harvester

International Nickel

International Paper

Johns-Manville

National Distillers

National Steel

Procter & Gamble

Sears Roebuck & Co

Standard Oil of California

Standard Oil (N.J.)

Texas Corporation

Union Carbide

United Aircraft

U.S. Steel

Westinghouse Electric

Woolworth

1959-1975

Allied Chemical

American Can

American Tobacco

Anaconda

Bethlehem Steel

Chrysler

Du Pont

Eastman Kodak

General Electric

General Foods

General Motors

Goodyear

International Harvester

International Nickel (name changed to Inco on April 21, 1976)

International Paper

Johns-Manville

Owen's-Illinois Glass

Procter & Gamble

Sears Roebuck & Co

Standard Oil of California

Standard Oil (N.J.) (name change to Exxon on November 1, 1972)

Swift & Co. (name changed to Esmark on May 30, 1930)

Texas Corporation (renamed Texaco in 1959)

Union Carbide

United Aircraft (name changed to United Technologies on May 1, 1975)

U.S. Steel

Westinghouse Electric

Woolworth

<u>1976-1978</u>

Allied Chemical

Aluminum Company of America

American Can

American Telephone & Telegraph

American Tobacco

Anaconda

Bethlehem Steel

Chrysler

Du Pont

Eastman Kodak

Esmark

Exxon

General Electric

General Foods

General Motors

Goodyear

International Harvester

Inco

International Paper

Johns-Manville

Minnesota Mining & Manufacturing

Owen's-Illinois Glass

Procter & Gamble

Sears Roebuck & Co

Standard Oil of California

Texaco

Union Carbide

United Technologies

U.S. Steel

Westinghouse Electric

Woolworth

1979-1981

Allied Chemical

American Can

American Tobacco

Bethlehem Steel

Du Pont

Eastman Kodak

Exxon

General Electric

General Foods

General Motors

Goodyear

International Business Machines

International Harvester

Inco

International Paper

Johns-Manville

Merck

Minnesota Mining & Manufacturing

Owen's-Illinois Glass

Procter & Gamble

Sears Roebuck & Co

Standard Oil of California

Texaco

Union Carbide

United Technologies

U.S. Steel

Westinghouse Electric

Woolworth

1982-1984

Allied Chemical (renamed Allied-Signal in 1985)

Aluminum Company of America

American Can

American Express

American Telephone & Telegraph

American Tobacco

Bethlehem Steel

Du Pont

Eastman Kodak

Exxon

General Electric

General Foods

General Motors

Goodyear

International Business Machines

International Harvester

Inco

International Paper

Merck

Minnesota Mining & Manufacturing

Owen's-Illinois Glass

Procter & Gamble

Sears Roebuck & Co

Standard Oil of California (renamed Chevron in 1984)

Texaco

Union Carbide

United Technologies

U.S. Steel

Westinghouse Electric

Woolworth

1985-1986

Allied-Signal Inc.

Aluminum Company of America

American Can

American Express

American Telephone & Telegraph

Bethlehem Steel

Chevron Corporation

Du Pont

Eastman Kodak

Exxon

General Electric

General Foods

General Motors

Goodyear

Inco

International Business Machines

International Harvester (renamed Navistar Internation Corp. In 1986)

International Paper

McDonald's Corporation

Merck & Company

Minnesota Mining & Manufacturing

Owen's-Illinois

Phillip Morris Companies

Procter & Gamble

Sears Roebuck & Co

Texaco

Union Carbide

United Technologies

U.S. Steel (renamed USX Corp. In 1986)

Westinghouse Electric

Woolworth

Allied-Signal Inc.

Aluminum Company of America

American Can (name changed to Primerica Corp. In 1987)

American Express

American Telephone & Telegraph

Bethlehem Steel

Boeing Co.

Chevron Corporation

Coca-Cola Co.

Du Pont

Eastman Kodak

Exxon

General Electric

General Motors

Goodyear

International Business Machines

International Paper

McDonald's Corporation

Merck & Company

Minnesota Mining & Manufacturing

Navistar Internation Corp.

Phillip Morris Companies

Procter & Gamble

Sears Roebuck & Co

Texaco

Union Carbide

United Technologies

USX Corp.

Westinghouse Electric

Woolworth

<u>1991-1996</u>

Allied-Signal Inc.

Aluminum Company of America

American Express

American Telephone & Telegraph (renamed AT&T Corp. In 1994)

Bethlehem Steel

Boeing Co.

Caterpillar Inc.

Chevron Corporation

Coca-Cola Co.

Disney

Du Pont

Eastman Kodak

Exxon

General Electric

General Motors

Goodyear

International Business Machines

International Paper

J.P. Morgan

McDonald's Corporation

Merck & Company

Minnesota Mining & Manufacturing

Phillip Morris Companies

Procter & Gamble

Sears Roebuck & Co

Texaco

Union Carbide

United Technologies

Westinghouse Electric

Woolworth

<u>1997-1998</u>

AT&T

Allied-Signal Inc.

Aluminum Company of America (name changed to Alcoa Inc. In 1999)

American Express

Boeing Co.

Caterpillar Inc.

Chevron Corporation

Coca-Cola Co.

Disney

Du Pont

Eastman Kodak

Exxon

General Electric

General Motors

Goodyear

Hewlett Packard

International Business Machines

International Paper

Johnson & Johnson

J.P. Morgan

McDonald's Corporation

Merck & Company

Minnesota Mining & Manufacturing

Phillip Morris Companies (Changed name to Altria in 2003)

Procter & Gamble

Sears Roebuck & Co

Travelers Group (name changed to Citigroup Inc. In 1998)

Union Carbide

United Technologies

Wal-Mart Stores

<u>1999-2003</u>

AT&T

Alcoa Inc.

Altria

American Express

Boeing Co.

Caterpillar Inc.

Citigroup

Coca-Cola Co.

Disney

Du Pont

Eastman Kodak

Exxon (changed name to Exxon Mobil Corp. In 1999)

General Electric

General Motors

Hewlett Packard

Home Depot

Honeywell International Inc.

Intel Corporation

International Business Machines

International Paper

Johnson & Johnson

J.P. Morgan (renamed J.P. Morgan Chase & Co. In 2001)

McDonald's Corporation

Merck & Company

Microsoft Corporation

Minnesota Mining & Manufacturing

Procter & Gamble

SBC Communications

United Technologies

Wal-Mart Stores

2004-2007

AT&T

American International Group

Alcoa Inc.

Altria

American Express

Boeing Co.

Caterpillar Inc.

Citigroup

Coca-Cola Co.

Disney

Du Pont

Exxon Mobil Corp.

General Electric

General Motors

Hewlett Packard

Home Depot

Honeywell International Inc.

Intel Corporation

International Business Machines

Johnson & Johnson

J.P. Morgan Chase & Co.

McDonald's Corporation

Merck & Company

Microsoft Corporation

Minnesota Mining & Manufacturing

Pfizer

Procter & Gamble

United Technologies

Verizon

Wal-Mart Stores

2008-2009

AT&T

Alcoa Inc.

American Express

Bank of America

Boeing Co.

Caterpillar Inc.

Chevron

Citigroup

Coca-Cola Co.

Disney

Du Pont

Exxon Mobil Corp.

General Electric

General Motors

Hewlett Packard

Home Depot

Intel Corporation

International Business Machines

Johnson & Johnson

J.P. Morgan Chase & Co.

Kraft Foods

McDonald's Corporation

Merck & Company

Microsoft Corporation

Minnesota Mining & Manufacturing

Pfizer

Procter & Gamble

United Technologies

Verizon

Wal-Mart Stores

Part 2

Year-to-Year Performance Comparison of PFCF vs. DJIA

Year	Price to Free Cash Flow	DJIA
1950	+31.13%	+17.62%
1951	+28.05%	+14.36%
1952	+16.88%	+0.51%
1953	+4.77%	+3.80%
1954	+64.80%	+43.96%
1955	+29.42%	+20.77%
1956	+13.86%	+2.27%
1957	+11.52%	-12.77%
1958	+52.66%	+33.96%
1959	+26.94%	+16.39%
1960	-15.20%	-9.34%
1961	+33.23%	+18.72%
1962	+12.12%	-10.81%
1963	+43.86%	-17.00%
1964	+18.81%	+14.57%
1965	+22.34%	-10.88%
1966	-9.40%	-18.94%
1967	+34.65%	+15.20%
1968	+6.99%	+4.26%
1969	-0.33%	-15.19%
1970	+31.82%	+4.82%
1971	+1.57%	+6.11%
1972	+27.32%	+14.58%
1973	+14.54%	-19.38%
1974	+19.51%	-25.05%
1975	+52.85%	+38.32%

YEAR	PRICE TO FREE CASH FLOW	DJIA
1976	+46.48%	+17.86%
1977	-1.77%	-17.26%
1978	+12.45%	-3.15%
1979	+18.57%	+4.19%
1980	+33.57%	+14.93%
1981	+10.62%	-9.23%
1982	+55.82%	+19.60%
1983	+35.23%	+20.26%
1984	+6.49$	-3.73%
1985	+35.77%	+27.66%
1986	+35.17%	+22.58%
1987	+34.19%	+2.26%
1988	+23.44%	+11.85%
1989	+35.96%	+26.96%
1990	-27.16%	-4.36%
1991	+99.09%	+20.32%
1992	+23.17%	+4.17%
1993	+34.21%	+13.72%
1994	+14.20%	+2.14%
1995	32.84%	+33.45%
1996	+21.72%	+26.01%
1997	+36.30%	+22.64%
1998	+37.71%	+16.10%
1999	+16.50%	25.22%
2000	+19.96%	-6.17%
2001	-3.91%	-7.10%
2002	-3.58%	-15.87%
2003	+28.96%	+23.98%
2004	+8.94%	+3.14%
2005	+3.41%	-0.11%
2006	+31.10%	+16.29%
2007	+16.72%	+6.37%
2008	-22.39%	-32.71%
2009	+22.95%	+15.43%

PART 3

Purchases made using "Price to Free Cash Flow" for the years 1950-2009

1950

American Smelting	40.60%
American Tobacco	-8.85%
Bethlehem Steel	+55.81%
Chrysler	+21.63%
Corn Products Refining	+1.35%
Du Pont	+43.53%
General Electric	+27.14%
General Foods	-0.90%
General Motors	+37.50%
Goodyear Tire & Rubber	+59.00%
International Harvester	+24.14%
Johns Manville	+2.27%
National Distillers	+29.50%
National Steel	+73.02%
Standard Oil of New Jersey	+41.69%
Union Carbide	+29.72%
U.S. Steel	+71.23%
Westinghouse Electric	+11.89%

1951

American Smelting	+38.23%
American Tobacco	+2.92%
Bethlehem Steel	+14.59%
Corn Products Refining	+8.42%
General Motors	+25.36%
Goodyear Tire & Rubber	40.85%
International Harvester	13.69%
Johns Manville	49.71%
Standard Oil of California	16.15%
Standard Oil of New Jersey	70.57%

133

1952

American Smelting	+2.64%
American Tobacco	+6.58%
Chrysler	+47.86%
Corn Products Refining	+9.72%
General Motors	+40.10%
International Harvester	-0.14%

1953

American Tobacco	+.038%
Bethlehem Steel	-2.26%
Corn Products Refining	+11.14%
Goodyear Tire & Rubber	+2.97%
International Harvester	-11.45%
United Aircraft	+27.84%

1954

American Smelting	70.07%
American Tobacco	12.60%
Bethlehem Steel	126.24%
Corn Products Refining	20.01%
Du Pont	59.53%
General Foods	33.42%
Goodyear Tire & Rubber	112.26%
International Nickel	74.97%
Standard Oil of California	51.30%
Standard Oil of New Jersey	59.92%
United Aircraft	77.48%
U.S. Steel	93.99%
Westinghouse Electric	50.60%

1955

American Smelting	+15.53%
American Tobacco	+31.16%
Bethlehem Steel	+55.22%
Corn Products Refining	+4.97%
Du Pont	+40.60%
General Foods	+26.92%
General Motors	+46.88%
Goodyear Tire & Rubber	+26.11%
International Harvester	+1.99%
International Nickel	44.83%

1956

American Smelting	+26.06%
American Tobacco	-3.99%
Corn Products Refining	+9.07%
International Harvester	+10.96%
International Nickel	+32.93%

1957

American Tobacco	+11.20%
Chrysler	-20.36%
Corn Products Refining	+20.68%

1958

American Tobacco	30.92%
Bethlehem Steel	50.58%
Corn Products Refining	63.50%
General Foods	52.89%
General Motors	53.73%
International Harvester	64.35%

1959

Allied Chemical	+27.44%
Anaconda	+8.87%
American Tobacco	+16.73%
Swift	+35.52%
International Harvester	+18.26%
Westinghouse	+54.81%

1960

Anaconda	-28.13%
American Tobacco	+24.74%
Chrysler	-42.22%

1961

Anaconda	+17.53%
American Tobacco	+58.19%
Chrysler	+30.34%
General Motors	+45.23%
International Harvester	+14.87%

1962

Anaconda	-11.57%
Chrysler	+53.32%
General Motors	+6.58%
International Harvester	+0.16%

1963

American Tobacco	+2.13%
Chrysler	+130.37%
General Motors	+40.43%
Johns Manville	+18.02%
U.S. Steel	+28.37%

1964

Anaconda	+17.11%
American Tobacco	+21.49%
Swift	+36.05%
International Harvester	+30.03%
Union Carbide	+8.38%
U.S. Steel	-0.23%

1965

Anaconda	+54.30%
American Tobacco	+21.43%
Johns Manville	+7.24%
U.S. Steel	+6.37%

1966

Johns Manville	-9.40%

1967

American Tobacco	-9.88%
Chrysler	+89.43%
General Motors	+31.39%
International Harvester	+7.9%

1968

Allied Chemical	-5.25%
American Tobacco	+23.11%
Chrysler	3.11%

1969

American Tobacco	-0.33%

1970

American Brands	+31.82%

1971

American Can	-10.50%
American Brands	-2.77%
Chrysler	+4.38%
International Harvester	+15.18%

1972

American Can	-0.60%
American Brands	+5.97%
Chrysler	+45.33%
General Motors	+5.00%
International Harvester	+33.81%
Alcoa	+25.90%
Standard Oil of California	+48.54%
Union Carbide	+23.08%
United Aircraft	+57.62%

1973

American Can	-10.04%
American Brands	-18.01%
Bethlehem Steel	+16.43%
General Motors	-37.66%
International Harvester	-29.25%
Standard Oil Of California	-8.45%
Union Carbide	-27.75%
United Aircraft	-42.58%
U.S. Steel	+26.25%

1974

American Can	+18.86%
American Brands	+1.18%
Union Carbide	+27.33%
United Aircraft	+44.95%
U.S. Steel	+5.25%

1975

American Can	+15.78%
American Brands	+24.99%
General Foods	+62.38%
General Motors	+98.46%
Goodyear Tire and Rubber	+76.85%
United Technologies	+48.05%
Westinghouse Electric	+43.77%

1976

American Can	+29.88%
American Brands	+25.07%
United Technologies	+71.51%
General Foods	+14.57%
Chrysler	+94.05%
General Motors	+41.00%
Westinghouse Electric	+39.04%
International Harvester	+56.84%
Standard Oil	+46.38%

1977

American Can	+5.13%
American Brands	+0.11%
Du Pont	-7.11%
General Motors	-12.90%
International Harvester	-3.18%

Standard Oil of California	+0.06%
United Technologies	-4.66%
Westinghouse Electric	+8.37%

1978

MMM	+33.66%
American Brands	+24.08%
Bethlehem Steel	+0.00%
Du Pont	+9.45%
Eastman Kodak	+18.78%
General Motors	-3.69%
Alcoa	+6.06%
Standard Oil of California	+28.62%
Westinghouse Electric	-2.91%

1979

American Brands	+41.94%
Bethlehem Steel	+12.74%
Du Pont	+1.88%
Eastman Kodak	-14.11%
General Foods	+9.90%
International Harvester	+13.72%
INCO	+55.24%
Alcoa	+20.16%
Standard Oil of California	+25.70%

1980

MMM	+22.19%
American Brands	+27.82%
Eastman Kodak	+50.75%
General Foods	-3.67%
Goodyear Tire and Rubber	+34.37%
INCO	-12.11%

Standard Oil of California	+81.64%
U.S. Steel	+50.57%
Owens Illinois	+32.15%
Westinghouse Electric	+52.03%

1981

American Brands	+2.45%
Bethlehem Steel	-5.78%
Goodyear Tire and Rubber	+26.88%
Alcoa	-8.67%
U.S. Steel	+2717%
Owens Illinois	+51.98%

1982

Goodyear Tire and Rubber	+91.05%
American Brands	+33.57%
General Foods	+31.73%
General Electric	+70.76%
Procter and Gamble	+51.98%

1983

American Can	+59.6%
American Brands	+35.97%
IBM	+30.33%
General Motors	+263.09%
General Electric	+27.06%
General Foods	+35.33%

1984

General Foods	+13.43%
U.S. Steel	-10.70%
General Motors	+9.14%
American Can	+13.92%

American Brands	+14.43%
Westinghouse Electric	-1.27%

1985

Westinghouse Electric	+74.07%
American Can	+22.55%
AT&T	+32.82%
Phillip Morris	+13.67%
General Motors	-4.15%
Inco	+8.68%
Union Carbide	+100.75%

1986

American Can	+45.04%
AT&T	+4.80%
Phillip Morris	+73.13%
Chevron	+25.31%
Westinghouse Electric	+27.58%

1987

Bethlehem Steel	+168.00%
IBM	-0.29%
Phillip Morris	+21.87%
Texaco	+12.20%
Union Carbide	+1.70%
USX Corp.	+43.95%
Westinghouse Electric	-8.34%

1988

Alcoa	+22.35%
AT&T	+10.93%
Bethlehem Steel	+38.81%

Boeing	+67.64%
Chevron	+21.51%
Texaco	+39.26%
General Motors	+44.20%
General Electric	+4.34%
Westinghouse Electric	+9.07%
United Technologies	+25.53%
USX Corp.	+2.35%
Union Carbide	+24.71%
Proctor and Gamble	+507%
Phillip Morris	+23.44%
International Paper	+13.24%

1989

Allied Signal	+12.85%
Alcoa	+36.25%
AT&T	+64.76%
Bethlehem Steel	-20.43%
Coca Cola	+75.80%
Union Carbide	-4.78%
General Motors	+7.96%
Phillip Morris	+67.18%
General Electric	+47.26%
Westinghouse Electric	+44.29%
Proctor and Gamble	+75.83%
International Paper	+24.58%

1990

Phillip Morris	+27.16%

1991

Goodyear Tire & Rubber	+202.76%
General Electric	+36.61%

Phillip Morris	+57.90%

1992

General Electric	+17.09%
Goodyear Tire and Rubber	+29.25%

1993

Boeing	+9.94%
Caterpillar	+67.09%
General Electric	++25.28%
General Motors	+71.18%
Goodyear Tire and Rubber	+34.62%
IBM	+21.77%
United Technologies	+32.78%
Westinghouse Electric	+10.99%

1994

Boeing	+10.98%
Caterpillar	+24.55%
Du Pont	+19.97%
General Motors	-21.78%
IBM	+32.88%
Phillip Morris	+8.04%
Union Carbide	+34.64%
United Technologies	+4.31%

1995

United Technologies	+53.92%
Allied Signal	+41.68%
Caterpillar	+7.39%
Union Carbide	+30.21%
Alcoa	+23.75%
General Motors	+26.29%

Goodyear Tire and Rubber	+37.17%
Eastman Kodak	+43.87%
Du Pont	+27.74%
General Electric	+44.00%
IBM	+25.68%
International Paper	+3.24%
Phillip Morris	+61.92%

1996

Phillip Morris	+29.06%
Allied Signal	+42.69%
United Technologies	+41.81%
Alcoa	+22.27%
Bethlehem Steel	-36.04%
Caterpillar	+30.64%
General Motors	+3.74%
Goodyear Tire and Rubber	+15.31%
IBM	+66.69%
International Paper	+11.56%
Union Carbide	+11.00%

1997

Caterpillar	+52.25%
IBM	+38.64%
General Motors	+12.00%

1998

General Motors	+21.82%
United Technologies	+56.60%

1999

Boeing	+28.72%

General Motors	+4.28%

2000

Boeing	+61.43%
Caterpillar	+3.39%
Eastman Kodak	-37.95%
General Motors	-27.17%
Phillip Morris	+100.09%

2001

Eastman Kodak	-20.31%
General Motors	-0.66%
Phillip Morris	+9.25%

2002

Boeing	-13.17%
Eastman Kodak	+25.17%
General Motors	-20.04%
Phillip Morris	-6.28%

2003

AT&T	-19.19%
Alcoa	+69.44%
Eastman Kodak	-23.46%
General Motors	+50.29%
Hewlett Packard	+33.54%
International Paper	+26.14%
McDonalds	+55.54%
Altria Group	+40.78%
SBC Communications	+1.22%
United Technologies	+55.33%

<u>2004</u>

AT&T	-1.43%
Eastman Kodak	+27.58%
Exxon Mobil	+27.61%
General Motors	-21.23%
Altria Group	+17.46%
SBC Communications	+3.64%

<u>2005</u>

Altria Group	+23.23%
AT&T	-4.69%
Exxon Mobil	+9.98%
General Motors	-53.38%
Hewlett Packard	+35.56%
Merck	-0.56%
Pfizer	-14.61%

<u>2006</u>

Altria	+14.47%
AT&T	+45.98%
Boeing	+26.19%
Caterpillar	+5.62%
Exxon Mobil	+25.82%
General Motors	+60.67%
Hewlett Packard	+40.68%
Honeywell	+21.55%
IBM	+17.83%
Merck	+34.07%
Pfizer	+9.51%
United Technologies	+10.75%
Walt Disney	+42.32%

2007

AT&T	+23.35%
Caterpillar	+20.83%
Exxon Mobil	+28.51%
General Motors	-15.48%
IBM	+11.13%
Merck	+32.00%
Pfizer	-13.54%
United Technologies	+21.86%

2008

Du Pont	-39.16%
Exxon Mobil	-13.46%
IBM	-18.34%
Pfizer	-18.59%

2009

AT&T	+4.22%
Boeing	+20.75%
Chevron	+3.73%
Du Pont	+34.10%
Exxon Mobil	-14.56%
General Electric	-1.56%
Hewlett Packard	+42.66%
Home Depot	+20.72%
IBM	+52.96%
Johnson & Johnson	+10.26%
Merck	+24.66%
Microsoft	+50.68%
MMM	+44.74%
Pfizer	+4.57%
United Technologies	+30.66%
Walt Disney	+38.72%

Part 4

Compounded return of $10,000 invested in 1950 in each would be worth

YEAR	PRICE TO FREE CASH FLOW	DJIA
1950	$13,113	$11,762
1951	$16,791	$13,451
1952	$19,625	$13,519
1953	$20,561	$14,032
1954	$33,884	$20,201
1955	$43,852	$24,397
1956	$49,930	$24,951
1957	$51,847	$21,765
1958	$79,150	$29,156
1959	$100,473	$33,935
1960	$85,201	$30,766
1961	$113,513	$36,525
1962	$127,270	$32,577
1963	$183,090	$38,115
1964	$217,529	$43,668
1965	$266,125	$48,420
1966	$241,109	$39,249
1967	$324,654	$45,215
1968	$347,654	$47,141
1969	$346,201	$39,981
1970	$456,362	$41,907
1971	$463,527	$44,468
1972	$590,163	$50,952
1973	$504,353	$41,077
1974	$602,752	$30,787
1975	$921,307	$42,585
1976	$1,349,530	$50,191
1977	$1,325,644	$41,527
1978	$1,490,687	$40,220
1979	$1,767,507	$41,904
1980	$2,360,859	$48,161

Year	Price-To-Free-Cash-Flow	DJIA
1981	$2,611,582	$43,716
1982	$4,069,367	$52,284
1983	$5,503,006	$62,877
1984	$5,860,151	$60,531
1985	$7,956,327	$77,274
1986	$10,754,726	$94,723
1987	$14,431,767	$96,864
1988	$17,814,573	$108,343
1989	$24,220,693	$137,552
1990	$30,799,033	$131,554
1991	$61,317,795	$158,287
1992	$75,525,128	$164,886
1993	$101,362,274	$187,510
1994	$115,756,717	$191,522
1995	$153,769,894	$255,586
1996	$187,168,715	$322,064
1997	$255,110,959	$394,980
1998	$351,313,302	$458,571
1999	$409,279,996	$574,233
2000	$490,972,284	$538,802
2001	$471,775,267	$500,548
2002	$454,885,713	$421,111
2003	$586,620,615	$522,093
2004	$639,064,498	$538,487
2005	$660,869,431	$532,500
2006	$866,433,448	$619,233
2007	$1,011,031,128	$658,492
2008	$784,873,128	$443,100
2009	$965,001,511	$511,470

Appendix C
Investing Goals Application (IGA)

The purpose of the IGA is to help individuals to understand what it will take to retire financially secure with enough income to live comfortably for as long as one lives. See chapter 26 for a more detailed explanation. Below are some screenshots of what we intend it too look like using the inputs provided.

It can vary dramatically based on each person's income level and expectations.

Inputs and Assumptions Page

Inputs and Assumptions	
When you see a ":" please enter input in column next to it.	
Date of Birth:	6/8/2000
Start Date:	6/14/2025
Age:	25
Year Started:	3
Current Income:	$30,000
Estimated Average Annual Income Growth:	4%
Estimated Average Annual Long-Term Inflation Rate:	3%
Estimated Average Annual Dividend Growth:	6%

401K Inputs	
Initial Annual % Contribution:	3%
Est. Ave. Fund Growth / Yr:	7%
Year of 1st % Contr. Increase:	2
Year of 2nd % Contr. Increase:	5
Year of 3rd % Contr. Increase:	10
Year of 4th % Contr. Increase:	12
Year of 5th % Contr. Increase:	15
Year of 6th % Contr. Increase:	18
Year of 7th % Contr. Increase:	20
Year of 8th % Contr. Increase:	22
Year of 9th % Contr. Increase:	23
Company % Match Contr.:	3%

Inputs and Assumptions	Page 2
When you see a ":" please enter input in column next to it.	
IRA Assumptions	
Year Started:	5
Est. Ave. Fund Growth / Yr:	8%
Initial Contribution:	2,500
Contribution Increase:	500
Year of 1st Contr. Increase:	8
Year of 2nd Contr. Increase:	12
Year of 3rd Contr. Increase:	15
Year of 4th Contr. Increase:	18
Year of 5th Contr. Increase:	21
Year of 6th Contr. Increase:	24
Year of 7th Contr. Increase:	27
Year of 8th Contr. Increase:	30
Year of 9th Contr. Increase:	32

Taxable Account Assumptions	
Year Started:	10
Est. Ave. Fund Growth / Yr:	8%
Initial Contribution:	3,000
Contribution Increase:	1,000
Year of 1st % Contr. Increase:	12
Year of 2nd Contr. Increase:	14
Year of 3rd Contr. Increase:	16
Year of 4th Contr. Increase:	18
Year of 5th Contr. Increase:	20
Year of 6th Contr. Increase:	22
Year of 7th Contr. Increase:	25

Dividend Reinvestment Assumptions	
Year Started:	15
Percent of Earnings Contributed:	5%
Annual Earnings Growth	4%
Dividend Yield (Beginning):	6%
Average Annual Dividend Growth Rate:	3%
Annual Appreciation Rate:	6%

Social Security Assumptions	
Average Current Benefit:	$20,000
Average Annual Inflation Rate:	3%

Retirement Income Assumptions	
Average Annual Dividend Increase:	6%
Estimated Dividend Yield:	3%

401K Accumulation

Est. Earnings	% Contr.	Tot. Contr.	Your Contr.	Growth	Cum. Tot.	Years	Age	Comp Match
30,000	3%	1,800	900	126	1,926	1	25	900
31,200	4%	2,184	1,248	288	4,398	2	26	936
32,448	4%	2,271	1,298	467	7,136	3	27	973
33,746	4%	2,362	1,350	665	10,163	4	28	1,012
35,096	5%	2,808	1,755	908	13,879	5	29	1,053
36,500	5%	2,920	1,825	1,176	17,974	6	30	1,095
37,960	5%	3,037	1,898	1,471	22,482	7	31	1,139
39,478	5%	3,158	1,974	1,795	27,435	8	32	1,184
41,057	5%	3,285	2,053	2,150	32,870	9	33	1,232
42,699	6%	3,843	2,562	2,570	39,283	10	34	1,281
44,407	6%	3,997	2,664	3,030	46,309+	11	35	1,332
46,184	7%	4,618	3,233	3,565	54,492	12	36	1,386
48,031	7%	4,803	3,362	4,151	63,446	13	37	1,441
49,952	7%	4,995	3,497	4,791	73,232	14	38	1,499
51,950	8%	5,715	4,156	5,526	84,476	15	39	1,559
54,028	8%	5,943	4,322	6,329	96,745	16	40	1,621
56,189	8%	6,181	4,495	7,205	110,131	17	41	1,686
58,439	9%	7,012	5,259	8,200	125,343	18	42	1,753
60,774	9%	7,293	5,470	9,285	141,921	19	43	1,823
63,205	10%	8,217	6,321	10,510	160,647	20	44	1,896
65,734	10%	8,545	6,573	11,843	181,036	21	45	1,972
68,363	11%	9,571	7,520	13,342	203,949	22	46	2,051
71,098	11%	9,954	7,821	14,973	228,876	23	47	2,133
73,941	11%	10,352	8,134	16,746	255,974	24	48	2,218
76,899	12%	11,535	9,228	18,726	286,235	25	49	2,307
79,975	12%	11,996	9,597	20,876	319,107	26	50	2,399
83,174	12%	12,476	9,981	23,211	354,794	27	51	2,495
86,501	12%	12,975	10,380	25,744	393,513	28	52	2,595
89,961	12%	13,494	10,795	28,490	435,498	29	53	2,699
93,560	12%	14,034	11,227	31,467	480,999	30	54	2,807
97,302	12%	14,595	11,676	34,692	530,286	31	55	2,919
101,194	12%	15,179	12,143	38,183	583,647	32	56	3,036
105,242	12%	15,786	12,629	41,960	641,394	33	57	3,157
109,451	12%	16,418	13,134	46,047	703,858	34	58	3,284
113,829	12%	17,074	13,660	50,465	771,398	35	59	3,415
118,383	12%	17,757	14,206	55,241	844,396	36	60	3,551
,123,118	12%	18,468	14,774	60,400	923,265	37	61	3,694
128,043	12%	19,206	15,365	65,973	1,008,444	38	62	3,841
133,164	12%	19,975	15,980	71,989	1,100,408	39	63	3,995
138,491	12%	20,774	16,619	78,483	1,199,664	40	64	4,155
144,031	12%	21,605	17,284	85,489	1,306,758	41	65	4,321
149,792	12%	22,469	17,975	93,046	1,422,272	42	66	4,494
155,784	12%	23,368	18,694	101,195	1,546,835	43	67	4,674
Totals		448,407	345,036	1,102,787	1,546,835			99,011
Estimated	Annual	Div.	Inc.	$46,405				

IRA Accumulation

Year	Contribution	Growth	Cum. Total		Age
1	0	0	0		1
2	0	0	0		2
3	0	0	0		3
4	0	0	0		4
5	2,500	200	2,700		5
6	2,500	416	5,616		6
7	2,500	649	8,765		7
8	3,000	941	12,707		8
9	3,000	1,257	16,963		9
10	3,000	1,597	21,560		10
11	3,000	1,965	26,525		11
12	3,500	2,402	32,427		12
13	3,500,	2,874	38,8014		13
14	3,500	3,384	45,685		14
15	4,000	3,975	53,660		15
16	4,000	4,613	62,273		16
17	4,000	5,302	71,575		17
18	4,500	6,086	82,160		18
19	4,500	6,933	93,593		19
20	4,500	7,847	105,941		20
21	5,000	8,875	119,816		21
22	5,000	9,985	134,8041		22
23	5,000	11,184	150,985		23
24	5,500,	12,519	169,004		24
25	5,500	13,960	188,465		25
26	5,500	15,517	209,482		26
27	6,000	17,239	232,720		27
28	6,000	19,098	257,818		28
29	6,000	21,105	284,923		29
30	6,500	23,314	314,737		30
31	6,500	25,699	346,936		31
32	7,000	28,315	382,251		32
33	7,000	31,140	420,391		33
34	7,000	34,191	164,582		34
35	7,000	37,487	506,069		35
36	7,000	41,046	554,115		36
37	7,000	44,889	606,004		37
38	7,000	49,040	662,044		38
39	7,000	53,524	722,568		39
40	7,000	58,365	787,933		40
41	7,000	63,595	858,528		41
42	7,000	69,242	934,770		42
43	7,000	75,342	1,017,111		43

Taxable Savings

Year	Contribution	Growth	Dividend	Cum. Total	Age
1	0				25
2	0				26
3	0				27
4	0				28
5	0				29
6	0				30
7	0				31
8	0				32
9	0				33
10	3,000	180	90	3,270	34
11	3,000	376	98	6,744	35
12	4,000	645	202	11,591	36
13	4,000	935	348	16,875	37
14	5,000	1,312	506	23,693	38
15	5,000	1,722	711	31,126	39
16	6,000	2,228	934	40,287	40
17	6,000	2,777	1,209	50,273	41
18	7,000	3,436	1,508	62,217	42
19	7,000	4,153	1,867	75,237	43
20	8,000	4,994	2,257	90,488	44
21	8,000	5,909	2,715	107,112	45
22	9,000	6,967	3,213	126,292	46
23	9,000	8,118	3,789	147,198	47
24	10,000	9,372	4,416	169,986	48
25	10,000	10,799	5,100	195,885	49
26	10,000	12,353	5,877	224,115	50
27	10,000	14,047	6,723	254,885	51
28	10,000	15,893	7,647	288,425	52
29	10,000	17,905	8,653	324,983	53
30	10,000	20,099	9,749	364,831	54
31	10,000	22,490	10,945	408,266	55
32	10,000	25,096	12,248	455,610	56
33	10,000	27,937	13,668	507,215	57
34	10,000	31,033	15,216	563,464	58
35	10,000	34,408	16,904	624,776	59
36	10,000	38,087	18,743	691,606	60
37	10,000	42,096	20,748	764,451	61
38	10,000	46,467	22,934	843,851	62
39	10,000	51,231	25,316	930,398	63
40	10,000	56,424	27,912	1,024,734	64
41	10,000	62,084	30,742	1,127,560	65
42	10,000	68,254	33,827	1,239,640	66
43	10,000	74,978	37,189	1,361,808	67
Totals	283,000	724,805	354,003		
Estimated	Annual	Dividend	37,189		

Dividend Reinvestment Accumulation (DRIP)

Year	Contribution	Dividend	Appreciation	Yr/End Bal.	Age
1	0				25
2	0				26
3	0				27
4	0				28
5	0				29
6	0				30
7	0				31
8	0				32
9	0				33
10	0				34
11	0				35
12	0				36
13	0				37
14	0				38
15	2.598			2,598	39
16	2.701	66	156	5,521	40
17	2.809	140	331	8,802	41
18	2.922	224	528	12,476	42
19	3.039	317	749	16,581	43
20	3.160	422	995	21,158	44
21	3.287	538	1,269	26,252	45
22	3.418	668	1,575	31,913	46
23	3.555	812	1915	38,195	47
24	3.697	972	2,292	45,155	48
25	3.845	1,149	2,709	52,858	49
26	3.999	1,345	3,171	61,373	50
27	4.159	1,561	3,682	70,775	51
28	4.325	1,801	4,247	81,147	52
29	4.498	2,064	4,869	92,579	53
30	4.678	2,355	5,555	105,167	54
31	4.865	2,675	6,310	119,017	55
32	5.060	3,028	7,141	134,246	56
33	5.262	3,415	8,055	150,978	57
34	5.473	3,841	9,059	169,350	58
35	5.691	4,308	10,161	189,510	59
36	5.919	4,821	11,371	211,621	60
37	6.156	5,384	12,697	235,858	61
38	6.402	6,000	14,151	262,412	63
39	6.658	6,678	15,745	291,491	63
14	6.925	7,416	17,489	323,320	64
40	7.202	8,225	19,399	358,146	65
41	7.490	9,111	21,489	396,236	66
42	7.789	10,080	23,774	437,880	67
Totals	137,581	89,415	210,884		
Estimated	Annual	Dividend	23,774		

157

Total Saving

Year	401K	IRA	Taxable	Drips	Cum. Tot.	Age
1	1,926				1,923	25
2	4,398				4,398	26
3	7,136				7,136	27
4	10,163				10,136	28
5	13,879	2,700			16,579	29
6	17,974	5,616			23,590	30
7	22,482	8,765			31,247	31
8	27,435	12,707			40,142	32
9	32,870	16,963			49,833	33
10	39,283	21,560	3,270		64,113	34
11	46,309	26,525	6,744		79,578/	35
12	54,492	32,427	11,591		98,510	36
13	63,446	38,801	16,875		119,122	37
14	73,232	45,685	23,693		142,611	38
15	84,473	53,660	31,126	2,598	169,259	39
16	96,745	62,273	40,287	5,521	199,305	40
17	110,131	71,575	50,273	8,802	231,978	41
18	125,343	82,160	62,217	12,476	269,721	42
19	141,921	93,593	75,237	16,581	310,751	43
20	160,647	105,941	90,488	21,158	357,076	44
21	181,036	119,816	107,112	26,252	407,964	45
22	203,949	134,801	126,292	31,913	465,043	46
23	228,876	150,985	147,198	38,195	527,060	47
24	255,974	169,004	169,986	45,155	594,965	48
25	286,235	188,465	195,885	52,858	670,584	49
26	319,107	209,482	224,115	61,373	752,703	50
27	354,794	232,720	254,885	70,775	842,399	51
28	393,513	257,818	288,425	81,147	939,756	52
29	435,498	284,923	324,983	92,579	4,045,404	53
30	480,999	314,737	364,831	105,167	1,160,567	54
31	530,286	346,936	408,266	119,017	1,285,488	55
32	583,647	382,251	455,610	134,246	1,421,509	56
33	641,394	420,391	507,215	150,978	1,569,000	57
34	703,858	461,582	563,464	169,350	1,728,905	58
35	771,398	506,069	624,776	189,510	1,902,243	59
36	844,396	554,115	691,606	211,621	2,090,117	60
37	923,265	6016,004	764,451	235,858	2,293,719	61
38	1,008,444	662,044	843,851	262,412	2,514,339	62
39	1,100,408	722,568	930,398	291,491	2,753,373	63
40	1,199,664	787,933	1,024,734	323,320	3,012,331	64
41	1,306,758	858,528	1,127,560	358,146	3,292,845	65
42	1,422,272	934,770	1,239,640	396,236	3,596,682	66
43	1,546,835	1,017,111	1,361,808	437,880	3,925,754	67

Estimated Social Security Income

Year	Age	Annual Benefit
42	66	67,198
43	67	69,214
44	68	71,290
45	69	73,429
46	70	75,632
47	71	77,901
48	72	80,238
49	73	82,645
50	74	85,124
51	75	87,678
52	76	90,308
53.	77	63,018
54	78	95,808
55	79	98,682
56	80	101,643

Estimated Retirement Income

Age	401K Yield	IRA Yield	Taxable Yield	DRIP Yield	Soc. Sec. Ben.	Total
60	25,332	16,623	18,743	7,782	0	68,571
61	27,698	18,180	20,748	8,745	0	75,371
62	30,253	19,861	22,934	9,700	0	82,748
63	33,012	21,677	25,316	10,744	0	90,749
64	35,990	23,638	27,912	11,887	0	99,427
65	39,203	25,756	30,742	13,136	69,214	174,078
66	42,668	28,043	33,827	13,530	71,290	185,267
67	46,405	30,513	37,189	13,936	73,429	197,258
68	49,189	32,344	39,421	14,354	75,632	206,599
69	52,141	34,285	41,786	14,785	77,901	216,425
70	55,269	36,342	44,293	15,229	80,238	226,765
71	58,585	38,522	46,951	15,686	82,645	237,645
72	62,100	40,834	49,768	16,156	85,124	249,096
73	65,826	43,284	52,754	16,641	87,678	261,150
74	69,776	45,881	55,919	17,140	90,308	273,840
75	73,963	48,634	59,274	17,654	93,018	287,202
76	78,400	51,552	62,830	18,184	95,808	301,275
77	83,104	54,645	66,600	18,729	98,682	316,096
78	88,901	57,923	70,596	19,291	101,643	331,710
79	93,376	61,399	74,832	19,870	104,692	348,159
80	98,979	65,083	79,322	20,466	107,833	365,492

Please Note: If inflation averages 3% over the long term (which it has until the most recent decade or two), an income of $70,000 today will equal about $228,343 in 2057 (when this example reaches age 65).

Looking at the projected income at the top, you can see why the Social Security Program is going to go broke unless it is modified in some way. There will not be enough coming into the program each year to pay all the retirees. I expect these numbers to either be reduced in size, for the required age to increase for future retirees or both. Who knows what Congress will do?

www.ingramcontent.com/pod-product-compliance
Lightning Source LLC
Chambersburg PA
CBHW081816200326
41597CB00023B/4277